Sibling, friend, lover—Jason Cusick explores all the dimensions of marital love in a way that will deepen relationships. Engagingly written and biblically based, I recommend this book for all who are married or contemplating marriage.

—Tremper Longman, professor, coauthor of *The Intimate Marriage Series*

For anyone questioning or looking to enhance their love—whether considering engagement, preparing for marriage, or already married—Jason Cusick has zeroed in on the three types of love taught in Scripture and experienced by couples. So many couples we see in therapy question their love when it changes from romantic to brother-sister love or friendship love. Reading *Love³* was a delightful encouragement to help couples embrace all expressions of love throughout their relationship journey.

—Dr. Clifford and Joyce Penner, authors of *The Gift of Sex and The Way to Love Your Wife*

# LOVE³

# LOVE³

## THREE ESSENTIALS
## FOR MAKING LOVE LAST

Jason Cusick

wesleyan
publishing
house

Indianapolis, Indiana

Copyright © 2011 by Jason Cusick
Published by Wesleyan Publishing House
Indianapolis, Indiana 46250
Printed in the United States of America
ISBN: 978-0-89827-465-3

Library of Congress Cataloging-in-Publication Data

Cusick, Jason.
  Love3 : three essentials for making love last / Jason Cusick.
     p. cm.
  Includes bibliographical references.
  ISBN 978-0-89827-465-3
  1. Love--Religious aspects--Christianity. I. Title. II. Title: Love 3. III. Title: Love three.

  BV4639.C87 2011
  248.8'44--dc22
                          2010029417

To Marie, my sister, my friend, my lover.

# CONTENTS

# ACKNOWLEDGEMENTS

I am the first to admit that when it comes to marriage, I am a novice. Writing a book on the essentials for a lasting marriage has been an act of idealistic passion mixed with a guarded fear of hypocrisy. I am humbly indebted to a greater community committed to living God's design for marriage.

I would like to thank the premarital mentoring team at Journey of Faith Church: Jan and Mitch, Kristie and John, Diana and John, Pam and Jim, Teri and Gene, Gail and Grant, Deborah and Jim, and Judy and Mike. I have learned so much from you. Thank you for taking the risk and responding to the call. Your ministry has made this book possible.

I would also like to thank the many pre-married, married, and struggling couples that have allowed me into their lives. I am grateful for the privilege you have given me to help you find healing in your relationships, and I apologize for the many times it was clear to you that I was (and still am) learning how to provide help to couples.

Special thanks to those who have encouraged me to write and those who have provided personal guidance and midcourse correction. Wayne, Teri, Judi, and Carol—thank you for keeping me centered. Clifford and Joyce Penner—thank you for helping revise the manuscript, as well as the personal help you've given Marie and me. Tremper Longman—thank you for your kind words. Rex Johnson—your direction and shepherding over the last ten years has meant the world to me. And Emily—thanks for your enthusiastic support and age-appropriate feedback.

Finally, thank you to my wonderful wife, Marie. Thank you for your patience and grace as I grow to be the man, husband, and father I am meant to be. I love you, Kitty.

# INTRODUCTION

love her."

"He loves me."

"We are in love."

What do these phrases mean?

What are we talking about?

I love Legos. I love my wife. I love God. Can I really use the same word for all of these? This limitation of language brings to the surface something much deeper about how we love. We love in different ways. Consider how to love your spouse at the following times: honeymoon night, wife's miscarriage, husband's only weekend off this month.

Love, but what kind? That's what this book is about.

Marie and I met in college. We were in biology class together. I noticed her legs; she noticed my lab partner. Our beginning was not a storybook romance.

A couple of weeks later, I noticed her Bible-verse-touting sweat-shirt (a spiritual turn-on for a new Christian convert like me) and struck up a conversation. As the semester went on, Marie and I began meeting after class to talk. Marie was very interested in a young man at church but was conflicted about her feelings for him. He seemed like a good candidate—he was a little older, seemed very devout; he was kind and funny, but there was no spark.

It didn't take much effort for me to turn my immediate atten-tion away from making her Mrs. Jason Cusick to listening and helping her talk through her feelings. We'd spend time talking about things we were learning, as well as sharing our spiritual struggles. We'd usually end our time together with a brief prayer for each other's week. We were spiritual brother and sister, pointing each other toward God and encouraging each other to walk by faith.

The school year progressed. We talked about other things that interested us—movies, hobbies, and fun things. I'd tell jokes; she'd laugh. She'd tell jokes and forget the punch lines. People in our class saw us become good friends while others wondered if there was more to our relationship.

One day, Marie remembered something she'd prayed for since childhood. "Dear Lord," her innocent, girlhood prayer began, "I would like a man who loves God more than me, someone who wants to serve you and others and, if it's not too much to ask . . . can he have blue eyes?" As I was sharing what I perceived to be some of my most sage advice and direction, she noticed my blue eyes. Something clicked, and her interest in me was sparked.

After three years of dating, we were married.

Love!

Five years into the marriage, it all came crashing down.

After counseling, prayer, and a lot of work, we moved through the darkness to a new relationship with each other. What happened? Where did the love go? Actually, the love was still there. But it was the wrong kind at the wrong times. Marie and I had something really good in the beginning and found something really good later, but we lost it in between.

At the beginning of our relationship, we got to know each other as spiritual brother and sister, nothing more. Our connection was based on our mutual submission to God and unselfish desire for the other's spiritual progress in life. As time went on, we formed a friendship. We did things together, joined our lives in shared activities, and built affection on our spiritual foundation. Only then did the romantic sensual bond begin.

When our marriage later hit rock bottom, the last place we could go was being lovers. Our friendship had suffered terrible blows as well. Instead, we had to start at the beginning—with our spiritual foundation in God. We recall praying separately: "God, if you want us together, we will commit ourselves to you and will trust you to build something new."

God built something new.

After fifteen years of marriage and three children, Marie and I are now honored to walk with other couples through the premarital process. We also have the opportunity to work alongside marriage mentors who help couples (and us) get to know God and one another as they grow closer. Whether you are dating or engaged, newly married or rediscovering the marriage you are in, my prayer is that the ideas contained in this book will help you as they have helped us.

Here's the main idea: Marriage consists of three relationships simultaneously. They are three different expressions of love. These three kinds of love correspond with three different Greek words for love. They are also the three love titles used by the most passionate couple in the Bible found in the epic love poem: Song of Songs.

| | |
|---|---|
| Brother and Sister | *agape*—selfless, spiritual love |
| Friend | *philia*—affinity, affection |
| Lover | *eros*—sexual, physical love |

This idea of the three loves is not new. Aristotle wrote about them as shared virtue, utility, and pleasure,[1] and C. S. Lewis later wrote about these loves in a context of Christian ethics.[2] I am intellectually indebted to both of these great thinkers.

I recommend reading the chapters in order, even though you may be interested in one chapter more than the other given your situation. Guys, for example, have probably already skimmed chapter 3 before making it to this introduction. Some of the strongest relationships have formed in the order this book presents—from spiritual to friendship to erotic love.

Let me also share a few words about divorce and remarriage. I don't mention the subject much here because my primary focus is on your current relationship. While focusing on marriage as a lifelong commitment, I in no way mean to cast judgment on those who have experienced divorce. My experience has taught me that those who are divorced are some of the greatest advocates for marriage and even greater advocates for exploring the strengths and growth areas of a new relationship before taking it to the next level.

*Love³* is about nurturing three kinds love. Couples are invited to experience the sacrificial love of God and model that in their relationship with each other. They are empowered to develop a full and fun friendship based on shared interests and mutuality. And, as they move into deeper layers of trust and commitment, they are encouraged to seal their love in the passionate fires of sexual love. The last chapter of the book explores what it means to move from one kind of love to the other as well as how to experience different loves at the same time. Marriage is like a dance in which we must learn about our own part and also how to move along graciously with another person. This takes time.

Mark Twain once said, "Love seems the swiftest, but it is the slowest of all growths. No man or woman really knows what perfect love is until they have been married a quarter of a century."[3] Marie and I have certainly not arrived. We are learning from our mistakes. We've been prideful about our love. We shut out friends when we should have allowed them in and let in some friends and family when they should have been kept out. Many people assumed we were fine when we were silently hurting.

Couples also need to be willing to work at love, and this means being willing to ask and answer hard questions. The kind of love people have nowadays is often too insulated and self-protective. Couples defend their love against perceived attacks even when the questions are necessary and intended to be helpful. Some couples also have an almost religious devotion to their love and reject attempts to improve it. This may have more to do with the chemicals that flood the brain when we form a new relationship than a true commitment to another person.

We need a new view of love, which is actually an old under-standing.

Love is about a selfless commitment to another person that is rooted in a spiritual bond. Love is about a being a companion in life with someone we enjoy. Love is about giving ourselves sexually to someone who we wildly and completely trust with our hearts. It is mature and thoughtful, not rash and rapturous. It's passionate, but not before its time. It is discovered and discerned within a community that encourages truth and commitment, not hidden and protected from inquiry like tragic romances.

We need love that is fueled by faith and friendship as well as fiery passion.

*God of Love,*

*You called us to love with a divine love that places you above all things and people. You have given us to each other for friendship, fellowship, and companionship. You awaken our passion, a fire of love that binds us as one in marriage. Help us discover the depths of your love for us and the love you have for our marriage.*

*In Jesus' Name,*
*Amen*

*1*

# BROTHER AND SISTER

Marriage creates a family relationship as real as
that between brother and sister.
—Craig Glickman[1]

*agape* [ah-gah-pey]: spiritual love; unselfish love; brotherly love
corresponding to the love of God for humankind.

> You have stolen my heart, my sister, my bride.
> —Song of Songs 4:9

I became a Christian in an African-American gospel church near South Central Los Angeles. Clapping, tambourines, dancing in the aisles, and hallelujahs were the normal Sunday experience. I went for the first time at the invitation of a friend, and I quickly realized how non-Christian (and white) I really was. Despite the cultural differences, I heard a message that changed my life, and the people in that congregation took me in as one of their own, as a brother.

In that church, everyone was related—Brother John, Sister Ada. I became Brother Jason. For them, the spiritual bond they had as Christians was stronger than the bonds they had with their families. When I married, they welcomed Sister Marie. It was then that I realized . . . I married my sister!

Calling people brother and sister who share the same spiritual beliefs is not unique to that congregation. Such spiritual kinship

goes back a long way. The Bible often uses family terms when referring to people of the same religious faith. Jesus challenged his own
family (and Jewish culture) when he used the family titles exclusively for people who followed his teachings (Mark 3:31–35). Our
spiritual relationship with each other comes before everything else,
even biological family.

In the romantic love poem of the Bible, Song of Songs, the royal
prince is captivated by the dark beauty of a young woman who, in
addition to many other terms of endearment, he calls his sister: "You
have stolen my heart, my sister, my bride" (Song 4:9).

Our sensibilities may be troubled or even offended by the use of
those titles side by side, but nothing was more romantic in the culture
in which the song was written. In ancient culture, brides were a matter
of contract; a sister was the person with whom a man shared his
heart. A woman may have a husband, but she was dedicated to her
brother.

My sister, my bride.

This is the best of both worlds! A bride is also a spiritual sister. She
shares the same beliefs and values as the groom. Together they share
the same faith in God. A groom is not only the one the bride will marry;
he is also her spiritual and emotional brother given by their creator.

> The emotional bonding modern Westerners expect as a mark of a healthy
> husband-wife relationship was normally characteristic of sibling relationships.
> —Joe Hellerman

The romantic lead in Song of Songs saw his future bride as his sister, culturally and spiritually. She was a daughter of Abraham. The door that opened up the potential for their relationship was that she was a spiritual woman—a woman of his own faith.

In marriage, our first and primary relationship with our spouse should be one of brother and sister in Christ. Before we are lovers and before we are friends, we need to be united in a spiritual partnership with God. Our love for each other should mirror God's love for us—a selfless, spiritual love that seeks the greatest good for the other person. The Greek word for this kind of love is *agape*.

It is the first and highest form of love.

## ARE YOU SPIRITUALLY COMPATIBLE?

There was once a charcoal burner who lived and worked by himself. A fuller, however, happened to come and settle in the same neighborhood; and the charcoal burner, having made his acquaintance and finding he was an agreeable sort of fellow, asked him if he would come and share his house. "We shall get to know one another better that way," he said, "and, besides, our household expenses would be diminished." The fuller thanked him, but replied, "I couldn't think of it, sir. Why, everything I take such pains to whiten would be blackened in no time by your charcoal."[2]

A fuller's job was bleaching cloth. His training, livelihood, and resources went into making things white. If I were a selfish charcoal burner, I would see great benefits in partnering with the fuller—all my stuff would be clean!

The point of this fable is: like will draw like. There are many reasons why men and women come together. They get along well, have common interests, or are physically attracted to each other. Some move in together to get to know each other better and save on finances (like the fable). But, underneath all of these commonalities, we need spiritual kinship. Are our lives built on the same foundation?

I recently enjoyed watching as a new building was erected on our church property. Each day I watched and imagined what it would be like to be in that building. I thought about what the rooms would look like and how lives would be changed by the teaching and relationships experienced there. But I quickly became frustrated by how long they spent on the foundation. I wanted to get in there and enjoy it. The construction company wanted to make sure it was built to last. Relationships are a lot like this. We want to get in there and enjoy it, but without the right foundation, big problems loom.

> For no one can lay any foundation other than the one
> already laid, which is Jesus Christ.
> —1 Corinthians 3:11

## WHAT IS SPIRITUAL INCOMPATIBILITY?

Imagine a farm in the 1800s—log cabin, horse-drawn wagon, and a young couple just starting out. The husband wants to plow a field for his crops. He gets the harness and chooses two animals to pull the plow: a sturdy ox and a strong-willed house cat. Even with only a basic understanding of farming, we quickly conclude our young husband doesn't know much. The two animals he has chosen are too different to work together. The ox and cat may get along well. They may even like similar things. As for the work the farmer wants to accomplish, they are incompatible.

This is the picture given in the Bible for spiritual incompatibility. It's like two different kinds of animals having a farming harness (a yoke) placed on them and being instructed to do a job. "Do not be unequally yoked [*heterozugeo*]," the apostle Paul wrote, warning Christians about partnering with people of other belief systems (2 Cor. 6:14 NKJV). When one person desires to shape his or her thinking, actions, and relationships to be more pleasing to Jesus Christ while the other does not, the two will eventually be drawn in opposite directions. They are spiritually incompatible.

When Jim and Lynn first met, they felt like they were cut from the same cloth. Both of them worked in medical sales, and they admired each other's determination and work ethic. Their relationship grew closer when they found themselves on the same team at their company's annual volleyball tournament. Jim saw Lynn's fun side, and Lynn saw how Jim loosened up and encouraged others on the team.

They decided to start seeing each other. Dinner dates and sporting events evolved into quiet walks on the beach and eventually an invitation by Jim for a weekend away.

"I don't think I can do that," Lynn said reservedly.

"I thought things were going well for us." Jim was confused.

"Things *are* going well between us, but I'm a Christian and that part of my life is really important to me."

"I'm fine with that, Lynn. I respect your beliefs. I know they bring meaning to you and that's important."

"But," Lynn said sheepishly, "I can't sleep with you."

"Why not?" Jim asked. "I feel really close to you, and I really care for you. Are you saying God doesn't want us to grow closer?"

"It's not that God doesn't want us to grow closer, it's just that the Bible says sex is for marriage."

"Lynn, I think I've been really cool about not doing things on Sundays with you because you want to go to church. And I even went to that Christian concert with you. What about my beliefs? I want this relationship to go further, so when are you going to start going along with what I believe?"

Jim and Lynn were going in different directions—something neither of them recognized until they were invested in each other. They felt emotionally and romantically compatible, but spiritually, they were not equally yoked.

> Regardless of the road that led them there,
> unequally yoked spouses all find they have common
> challenges, problems, and concerns.
> —Lee and Leslie Strobel

Sometimes two people of the same religion can also be spiritually incompatible. Maybe they are at different spiritual speeds or come from very different traditions within the same religion. Frank and Lila found this to be their challenge. Frank was from a Baptist tradition; Lila was from a more charismatic faith. For Frank, faith was about understanding and applying the Word of God—the Bible. Lila, while committed to the Bible, had a passion for allowing the Holy Spirit to guide her daily life with God. These different traditions mirrored their personalities as well. They found it difficult to talk about spiritual things, pray together, or even agree on a church that met their spiritual needs. They both agreed that they loved and served the same God, but spiritual compatibility was a big issue. Spiritually, they were out of sync.

> Here we are, you and I, and I hope a third, Christ, is in our midst.
> —Aelred of Rievaulx

Another form of incompatibility comes when one partner, because of new spiritual zeal, becomes so religious that it endangers the relationship. This is common when people are first converted to a faith. Being new to your faith is like when you first meet someone and start dating. You think about them all the time, talk about them all the time, and try to spend every waking moment with them—usually to the detriment of other relationships in your life. When you first find faith, it feels like you are catching up on something you had been missing out on. Ideally, as your faith matures, you find a mature and practical expression of what you believe that helps to make all your relationships better. Wisdom says to allow space for your faith to mature before growing deeper in a romantic relationship.

Spiritual compatibility should be a priority when partnering with people, especially when it comes to marriage. The closer you plan on getting to someone, the more this should be explored. What do you both believe about God, life, truth, and the world? When considering marriage, a good question to ask is, "Who do I love more: God or my partner?" If you have different answers, there is a problem.

## CONVERTS, HYBRIDS, OR SOMETHING ELSE?

What do couples do when they are spiritually incompatible? One pastor humorously said, "When a man and woman get married, they make a commitment to become one. Then they spend the rest of their lives arguing about which one it is going to be!" Going on an assumption that faith and spirituality are important to one or both people in the relationship, statistics on interfaith marriages say that many couples resolve the tension of different religions by one partner converting to the other partner's faith.[3] The general rule of thumb is—the more exclusive the person's beliefs, the more pressure there will be for the other person to convert. Sometimes couples believe they have reached a compromise with regard to their different religious beliefs, but the primacy of their deep convictions may lurk underneath.

"Suzi and I have decided to get married!" Marc said.

"So you've worked through your spiritual differences?" I asked.

Marc was attending an evangelical Christian church, and Suzi was raised Catholic.

"Yeah," Suzi said. "We've been going to Marc's church Sunday mornings and the Catholic church at night, but I've been getting much more out of the services at his church. When we get married, I'm going to make Marc's church my church."

I paused before dropping the bomb.

"If you were going to have children," I asked, "how would you raise them?"

"Oh, we'll raise them Catholic," Suzi said without hesitation.

Marc was stunned. Apparently, Suzi's convictions went deeper than he had realized.

> When children arrive, buried beliefs resurface.
> —Dugan Romano

Couples that don't resolve spiritual incompatibility by conversion find themselves with other solutions. Some couples try practicing both faiths together, while others practice their faiths side by side, looking for common beliefs and traditions they can share. This can be a rich experience when it works. Other couples resolve their differences by stopping the practice of their faiths altogether. Sadly, spiritual incompatibility most often causes couples to grow apart, not together. God's design is that devotion to our Creator would take a primary place in our marriage, not that it would have to be accommodated or removed because it interferes with our love for each other.

## FROM BEING COMPATIBLE TO BEING GOD-CENTERED

No matter where a couple is in their spiritual compatibility, being married changes things.

One ancient writer referred to marriage as a "vocational change" that necessitates changes in one's faith. My wife and I have always struggled with regular times of Bible reading and prayer together as a couple. It took us a while to figure out that not only do we learn and pray very differently, but also "quiet time" (as many Christians call it) had some very negative baggage for her from long before we met.

> Spiritual transparency involves revealing to your spouse the nature and essence of your ongoing relationship with God.
> —Brian Nystrom

When two people marry, God begins to form them into one. We are invited to find a way to experience God together. This involves creativity and compromise. We need to do more than get along spiritually. We need our spiritual life to shape our marriage. This makes marriages happy and strong. Les and Leslie Parrot say: "When researchers examined the characteristics of happy couples who had been married for more than two decades, one of the most important qualities they found was 'faith in God and spiritual commitment.'"[4]

Being brother and sister means we place God at the center of our relationship. As we individually grow closer to God, we grow closer to each other, as illustrated by the following figure.

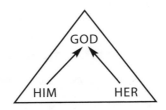

This three-way relationship keeps our focus in the right place. First, it prevents us from looking to our spouse to meet our deepest needs. Some couples struggle with spousal idolatry. This is when we place our spouse in the highest position—a position reserved for God. God does not expect our deepest needs to be met by other people or things. Until we learn to love God, we cannot love our spouse as God intends. Second, it reminds us that our primary marriage commitment is to God, not our spouse. I spoke with a man recently who was tempted to cheat on his wife. He said that the deciding factor was not how his wife was treating him, but that on his wedding day he made a commitment to God to be faithful. With all the needs and desires we possess, we need a commitment that transcends human loyalty. As brother and sister, our ultimate loyalty is to our Father.

Sheila was excited to be engaged to a Christian man. She experienced a painful divorce and worked hard as a single mom. Steve came into her life, and her life changed for the better. But she hit a spiritual wall during their premarital mentoring at church. She had been raised in church and attended services off and on over the years. She prided herself on being a good Christian woman, but inwardly she knew she was sitting on the fence. "I felt like God said to me, 'Sheila, you're either in or you're out. No more playing around.' I was marrying a man that wanted to place God first in our relationship, and I had to make a decision. Was I going to put God first or not?"

Sheila made an important decision. She put God at the top of that triangle and committed to grow in her personal relationship with Christ. At their wedding ceremony, Steve and Sheila mixed three colors of sand together, symbolizing their union as a couple with God.

As they grow spiritually, they will share struggles, victories, and prayers and become spiritually transparent with each other. They will work to break down barriers that prevent honesty and openness. They will grow in caring for each other as spiritual siblings as well as husband and wife. This is the kind of spiritual unity the Bible celebrates when it refers to married couples as "equal partner[s] in God's gift of new life" (1 Pet. 3:7 NLT).

> We allow marriage to point beyond itself when we accept two central missions: becoming the people God created us to be, and doing the work God has given us to do.
> —Gary Thomas

As we become God-centered, we allow God to meet our emotional needs. We grow to understand that we are valuable to God and gifted for wonderful things in the world. Our spouse gets the overflow of our God-centered life. Being God-centered means that I learn what it means to be self-controlled and aware of my good desires as well as my selfish desires. As I trust God to meet my needs in the right ways and at the right times, my spouse experiences the overflow of my God-centered life.

## RETHINKING SIBLING RIVALRY

The first place we learn how to relate to others is our own homes. My wife and I have always tried to encourage our children to love one another. Marie will say, "Go talk to Brother Asa" or "Can you help Sister Elia?" In Marie's Vietnamese culture, everyone has a kinship title. Like the African-American church mentioned earlier, kinship terms are social cues that remind us how we are related to each other. More importantly, they remind us how we should treat each other. I am supposed to refer to my wife as "em" (which in Vietnamese means "little sister").

Gary Thomas writes, "When I realized I am married to *God's daughter*—and that you, women, are married to *God's sons*—everything about how I view marriage changed overnight. If you want to change your marriage, extend this analogy and spend some time thinking about God as Father-*in-law*. Because he is!"[5]

What does it look like to love your husband or wife as a brother or sister? First and foremost, we express a spiritual love for our partner. Some relationships begin on a sensual or sexual basis. But God's love is a family love—a love that seeks the best for the other person. This spiritual love is so primary that the Bible acknowledges times in a marriage when husbands and wives may temporarily abstain from sexual intimacy in order to focus themselves on prayer and their relationship with God (1 Cor. 7:5). This is not to say that sex and spirituality are incompatible. Just the opposite! If we are not careful, great sex may give us the appearance that we are more spiritually bonded than we actually are. We'll explore this more in chapter 3.

> Treat younger men as brothers . . . and younger
> women as sisters, with absolute purity.
> —1 Timothy 5:1–2

Loving each other as brother and sister in Christ is the most pure form of love. It is a love that seeks the other's good and challenges our selfishness. This kind of love says, "I'm family, so I'm going to be honest with you." The Bible encourages Christians to think about the conscience and sensitivities of others, rather than focusing on one's own rights (Rom. 14; 1 Cor. 8). In a marriage of spiritual siblings, this means that we don't allow our strengths to override our spouse's weaknesses. If it is a nonessential matter, we compromise rather than offend, divide, or cause someone to violate his or her conscience. *Agape* love is grounded in compassion. This kind of love is not primarily expressed in feelings but in concrete actions.

## A VERB FOR SPIRITUAL SIBLINGS

First Corinthians 13 is a common Bible reading at weddings. It is the Bible's explanation of love: "Love is patient, love is kind" (1 Cor. 13:4). But this passage wasn't written for husbands and wives; it was originally written to a profoundly dysfunctional group of Christians by the founder of their congregation. These spiritual brothers and sisters were acting like selfish, bratty children in a dysfunctional home, not the spiritual children of a loving heavenly Father. Consider the following translation.

Love never gives up.
Love cares more for others than for self.
Love doesn't want what it doesn't have.
Love doesn't strut,
Doesn't have a swelled head,
Doesn't force itself on others,
Isn't always "me first,"
Doesn't fly off the handle,
Doesn't keep score of the sins of others,
Doesn't revel when others grovel,
Takes pleasure in the flowering of truth,
Puts up with anything,
Trusts God always,
Always looks for the best,
Never looks back,
But keeps going to the end. (1 Cor. 13:4–7 MSG)

Each line contains a verb, not a feeling. Love is about doing. It is about acting like brothers and sisters. Many husbands and wives become preoccupied with feelings, passions, and desires. They neglect their primary obligation to love each other with the self-less love of spiritual siblings, children of the same loving God. In my office, I have each line from 1 Corinthians 13 magnetized on a board. I ask couples to reorder the list, prioritizing which expressions of love they need to work on with their spouse. Spiritual love is about doing loving things to and for each other because this is the Father's desire.

> I don't believe an accident of birth makes people sisters or brothers. It makes them siblings, gives them mutuality of parentage. Sisterhood and brotherhood is a condition people have to work at.
> —Maya Angelou

## FROM DATING TO MARRIAGE

In order to express spiritual love, we need to have a relationship with God. The progression of having a relationship with God is similar to the progression of a romantic relationship. It begins with meeting for the first time. Maybe you saw God from across a crowded room. Perhaps you knew God from the neighborhood growing up. When you first meet someone, you do not know them. You may know about them; you may even know some details about them, but you don't *know* them. Some people hear about God in popular culture; others know people that know God. Still others maybe grew up going to church with their parents. At some point, you make a decision that you want to get to know God more. This is when dating comes in.

Dating God is when you get together to get to know each other. You may go out once a week. You go to church, serve at some local outreach, or listen to a message on the radio. Maybe you talk to your friends about God. "So what's God really like?" you ask. You find out the kind of things that interest God to see if you are similar. You realize that some of the things you thought were true were just rumors. You may be dating other gods during this time. You are asking questions and playing the religious field. But eventually, you realize that you are thinking about God more than other things. You realize you need to get serious.

It used to be called "going steady." Now people change their "relationship status." It is when the relationship is exclusive. Now you are thinking about commitment. "Could I see myself with God for the rest of my life?" you ask. You start counting the cost. You think about the things you'd be giving up living as a spiritual single. You are taking seriously the things God has been saying. You make some new friends, and they think you and God are a good match. Other friends think you are crazy. In your heart, you get to a point of no return. You are being pulled, called, betrothed. Betrothed? It means engaged. Or, at least, you have been asked. You know God is asking for a commitment, and you are feeling a yes or a no.

There comes an important point in a person's life when a special ceremony takes place. There are no flowers, rings, or photographer. It's a ceremony of the heart, when God says, "I have created you, given my life for you, and have great plans for you. Will you open your heart to me and let me lead you in this life?" We are at the altar and invited to say, "I do." Much like a romantic relationship, God wants our hearts. It is a decision that not only changes what our lives are about, but also our ability to love others the way God loves them. When we have committed our lives to God, we begin to understand what it means to have covenant love in a relationship, the kind of love God wants us to experience in marriage.

## COVENANT OR CONTRACT?

We are contract culture—cell phones, rental property, credit agreements—we strike a deal, agree on terms, and then expect commitment. What happens when one party doesn't deliver?

No one gets married thinking that they will back out if the other person does not deliver, but when tough times come, many of us are tempted to revisit the rights and responsibilities of our marriage agreement. When the tough times came in our marriage, God let Marie and I know that we do not have a marriage contract; we have a marriage covenant.

A covenant marriage . . . is rooted in a promise that two people make in the presence of God and other witnesses. In a covenant marriage each person vows to give their total being first to God and then to the other.
—Jim and Sarah Sumner

Marriage covenants are spiritual agreements between two parties and God. They are unconditional. This means that each person makes a commitment to love the other regardless of the other's behavior. These are the kinds of covenants God made most often in the Bible. God made a promise to give Noah protection from destruction (Gen. 6–9), Abram the Promised Land (Gen. 15), and David an everlasting kingship (2 Sam. 7). In the New Testament, the new covenant is God's promise of eternal life (John 3:16). What did God ask of Noah, Abram, and David in return? Simply that they would believe and receive the gift of love. Many people confuse Jesus' new covenant with a contract. They think God agrees to grant forgiveness and heaven in exchange for a life of good works and humility. Instead, God unconditionally grants forgiveness and heaven. When we believe and receive this for ourselves, we unconditionally respond with good works and humility.

Marriage is to be a picture of God's love toward us—*agape*. It is one way. You love the other person regardless of any response to you. Each person in the marriage unconditionally gives his or her life and love to the other, only asking the other to believe and receive. Being brother and sister in Christ means we take what we know about God's love to us and give it to each other. We do not demand things from each other; we give like God does. The Bible even encourages couples to see the relationship between Christ and the church as a model for marriage.

Out of respect for Christ, be courteously reverent to one another.

Wives, understand and support your husbands in ways that show your support for Christ. The husband provides leadership to his wife the way Christ does to his church, not by domineering but by cherishing. So just as the church submits to Christ as he exercises such leadership, wives should likewise submit to their husbands.

Husbands, go all out in your love for your wives, exactly as Christ did for the church—a love marked by giving, not getting. Christ's love makes the church whole. His words evoke her beauty. Everything he does and says is designed to bring the best out of her, dressing her in dazzling white silk, radiant with holiness. And that is how husbands ought to love their wives. They're really doing themselves a favor—since they're already "one" in marriage. (Eph. 5:21–28 MSG)

## WHAT (OR WHO) IS OUR MARRIAGE ABOUT?

I asked Mitch and Jan, a couple I deeply respect, about how their spiritual lives tie into their marriage. This was their response:

> We tend to think of ourselves as teammates and our ultimate goal is to live our lives in such a way that we help lead others to Christ. Our children became a part of this team at an early age and are effective evangelists in their own right. We have a photo frame with multiple pictures in it and a saying in one slot that has been our family mission statement: "Lord, make our family a testimony of your faithfulness, an extension of your love, and a witness of your Son to this generation."
>
> So by having a common goal, a wide range of other issues in life fall into place—commitment that marriage is forever, priority of family, approach to world affairs and pop culture, use of money and time, confidence in eternity, etc. I don't mean to make it sound boring because we are still crazy about each other, but the less time and effort spent on debating issues and conflict, the more time can be spent enjoying life together and being productive servants.[6]

Many people marry someone to find fulfillment, have pleasure, or raise a family. Shouldn't marriage be about something bigger than all these? Two people come together with gifts, abilities, talents, time, resources, and passion for each other. It is tragic if that relationship's ultimate end is to feed only itself. Marriage is meant for something bigger—something eternal!

In the book *Mixed Ministry: Working Together as Brothers and Sisters in an Oversexed Society*, the authors refer to Christians as "sacred siblings." They highlight five ultimate pursuits and responsibilities that I believe translate well into mutual commitments for couples seeking a spiritual foundation for their marriage.

1. We Are All Called to Know Jesus—addressing our own need for forgiveness and salvation is what begins the spiritual life. As couples, we start and return to this place regularly.

2. We Are All Called to Grow Up—committing to a path to grow in our spiritual and emotional maturity. As couples, we commit to growing in knowledge and grace.

3. We Are All Called to Share Life's Tasks—partnering together in life's challenges and responsibilities. As couples, we find the roles that help us be the most effective.

4. We Are All Called to Obedience—encouraging each other to be morally, ethically, and spiritually accountable to God. As couples, we pursue truth over personal gain.

5. We Are All Called to Serve—seeing the great needs of the world we work as a complementary team. As couples, we empower one another to be a blessing to others. [7]

A marriage based on *agape* love has these five pursuits at its foundation. Loving each other as brother and sister is the highest form of love. When friendship and romantic love are built on its foundation, a relationship begins in which all things are possible.

## JON AND SARAH'S STORY

What does a spiritual partnership in marriage look like? We need not go further back than the nineteenth century in colonial New England. It is here that we find a marriage that produced an influential family legacy that eventually included thirteen college presidents, sixty-five professors, one hundred lawyers, sixty-five physicians, and eighty holders of public office. [8] Jonathan Edwards, who would become one of the best known revivalist preachers of the Great Awakening, met his spiritual match in the young and beautiful Sarah. He would be best known for his sermon, "Sinners in the Hands of an Angry God," but what few people know is that there is one subject he wrote and preached about more than any other: love.

It was their faith that united Jon and Sarah because, in every other way, they were complete opposites. Jon was awkwardly tall, shy, bookish, and socially introverted. He possessed all the attributes that come with intellectual brilliance. Sarah was gifted in conversation, charming, and had that great ability of putting others at ease. It was her love and devotion for the "great Being" that caught Jonathan's eye and attracted him to Sarah. Their relationship would go down in religious history as one of the great spiritual marriages of all time.

> A sweeter couple I have not seen. . . . She . . . talked feelingly and solidly of the things of God, and seemed to be such a helpmeet to her husband, that she caused me to . . . [pray] to God, that he would send me a daughter of Abraham to be my wife.
> —George Whitefield

What was their secret?

If you were to ask them what brought them together, helped them through the ups and downs of marriage, and empowered them to influence so many lives, they would have undoubtedly pointed to a divine source. Elisabeth Dodds, in telling the story of Jonathan and Sarah's life together, refers to God as the "Central Fact" of their lives.[9]

## THEY LOVED IN TANGIBLE WAYS

Jon and Sarah showed God's love to each other in practical ways. For them, God's character was not an abstract thing but something that could be experienced. If you were to have asked Jon what he believed about love, he likely would have said, "Look at the way I relate to God, my wife, and family." For him, love was incarnational—an idea made tangible in real life. He showed kindness and respect to his wife. He would share his heart and mind with her, seeking her advice and direction.

> Happy are the couples who do recognize and understand that their happiness is a gift of God, who can kneel together to express their thanks not only for the love which he has put in their hearts, the children he has given them, or all of life's joys, but also for the progress in their marriage which he brings about through the hard school of mutual understanding.
> —Paul Tournier

## THEY EXPERIENCED GOD TOGETHER

They also worshiped God together. Singing was Jonathan Edwards' picture of an ideal society, and the Edwards family made this part of their home life. But singing was not their only form of worship. Their home was characterized by prayer and Bible reading. At breakfast and after supper, Jonathan would pray and share Scripture. After the children were in bed, Sarah would go into Jon's study where they would talk and pray for each other. Their devotion to God often took them outdoors. Leaving his studies during the day, they would take horseback rides. Their conversations were rich and robust but sometimes, as Dodds puts it so eloquently, "they would simply jog along without speaking, but communicating."[10]

## THEY PRAYED AND SUPPORTED EACH OTHER

The Edwardses sought God in tough times. Life in eighteenth-century New England was hard. Their Puritan upbringing and culture could be demanding. They had a large family to nurture. Jonathan's greatness was accompanied by personal challenges of stress, time constraints, and a certain absentmindness. Sarah, while blessed with resilience, struggled with being accepted by others and having the approval of God and her husband. Her sense of worry culminated in a crisis point in her life. Jonathan listened to her struggles, and using his unique gifts, walked her through the crisis. They entrusted themselves to each other and cared for each other as spiritual siblings through life's challenges.

> Our earthly marriage is temporary, but our spiritual relationship . . .
> our brotherhood and sisterhood in Christ . . . *that* relationship is forever.

Jon and Sarah had a love of an eternal quality. At Jonathan's untimely death, Sarah wrote to her daughter saying she believed God had taken her husband. Though covered by a dark cloud, she said that God had her heart and by having Jonathan as long as she did, she found herself thanking God for his goodness.

Jonathan Edwards—the great intellectual, revivalist, and scholar—of all the subjects and ideas he could have reserved for his parting words, spoke of his marriage to his spiritual sister: "Give my kindest love to my dear wife, and tell her that the uncommon union which has so long subsisted between us has been of such a nature as I trust is spiritual and therefore will continue forever."[11]

*Heavenly Father,*

*Help us not to see the terms* brother *and* sister *as a romantic buzz kill, but as an invitation to a much deeper, more intimate form of love, the kind of love that you have for us—forgiving, holy, and life changing. Help me point my partner toward you. Together, may we learn to love you, so we can express that* agape *love to each other. By faith in your Son, may we enjoy a spiritual partnership that will stretch into eternity.*

*In Jesus' Name,*
*Amen*

# DISCUSSION STARTERS

1. What do you believe was the most important part of this chapter?

2. After reading this chapter, what do you and your loved one have different beliefs about? In what areas are your beliefs and values similar?

3. List the following things in order of importance: work or career, family, God, personal growth, church participation, recreation or hobbies. Compare your lists with each other. Discuss the similarities and differences.

4. After reading this chapter, do you believe you are equally yoked? Why or why not? If you are not, discuss the future of your relationship in light of this important difference.

5. How would you describe your personal relationship with Jesus Christ: know him from a distance? Just met? Dating infrequently? Going steady? Engaged? Married and faithful? What does (or would) a marriage relationship with Jesus Christ look like in your life?

## LOVE IN ACTION

1. For the next week, take time daily to pray for each other together. Find a quiet place, ask each other for areas of concern, struggle, and celebration. After listening to each other's prayer requests, take turns praying for the issues you discussed. Spend specific time asking God to guide your relationship.

2. On page 39 is the description of *agape* love according to 1 Corinthians 13. On a separate piece of paper, make two columns. In the left column, write each line of the verse. In the second column, write out a very practical or daily way you could put into action this verse for your partner.

   Take the following as an example. In the first column would be: Love isn't always me first; in the second: I will ask my partner's opinions and thoughts before sharing my own.

3. The Bible says we should love one another as God loves us. Read Psalm 103. Make a list of the different ways God shows his love to us. Then make a list of ways you can imitate God's love with your partner.

4. Attend a Bible-teaching church with each other on a weekly basis. If you do not already have one, find a church home where you can connect with other couples like yourself and grow in your understanding of God and the Bible.

# RECOMMENDED READING

*Covenant Marriage: Building Communication & Intimacy* by Gary Chapman

*Devotions for a Sacred Marriage: A Year of Weekly Devotions for Couples* by Gary Thomas

*Just How Married Do You Want to Be?: Practicing Oneness in Marriage* by Jim and Sarah Sumner

*Surviving a Spiritual Mismatch in Marriage* by Lee and Leslie Strobel

# FRIENDS

Happy marriages are based on a deep friendship.
—John Gottman[1]

philia [fi-lee-ah]: friendship love; affinity;
to have feelings of affection for; an associate

> "This is my lover, this is my friend."
> Song of Songs 5:16

I was crushed. I was seven years old, and my friend Vinh told me that someone else was his best friend. I came home that night and asked my dad if I could talk to him after dinner. We lay on my parents' bed, and I presented my lonely tale.

"I don't have a best friend anymore," I said.

"Sometimes we don't have a *best* friend," he replied.

"Do you have a best friend?" I asked him.

"I have a few good friends," he said, "but your mom is my best friend."

That conversation helped shape my understanding of friendships. I accepted that I, too, would probably only have a few good friends. I also concluded that when it was time to look for a wife, I should look for someone I could see as my best friend.

In addition to using the terms *brother* and *sister* to refer to their relationship, the couple in Song of Songs also refers to each other as friends. The groom writes, "This is my lover, this my friend" (Song 5:16).

Marie and I began our relationship with a firm spiritual commitment to God. We see ourselves as sacred siblings of the same spiritual parent, and then we are best friends. Before we realized that we were dating and becoming exclusive, we talked for hours, learned about each other, had disagreements, and worked to resolve them. We did things together and supported each other through difficulties. This was without romantic expression or sexual involvement. It was a friendship.

> Gallup's research indicates that a couple's friendship quality could account for 70 percent of overall marital satisfaction.
> —Tom Rath

In marriage, the second relationship we should have with our spouse should be that of friends. Building on a spiritual foundation and before we are lovers, we need to enjoy the companionship of a strong friendship. Our love should be expressed in fondness and affection for someone with shared interests, someone who, if the passions of attraction were not present, we would likely find ourselves spending time with anyway. The Greek word for this kind of love is *philia*.

It is the stuff of great marriages.

## WHAT IS A FRIEND?

In the television series *Boston Legal* (2004–2008), Denny Crane and Alan Shore were shrewd lawyers who enjoyed all the affluence their profession provided. While the show pushed the envelope of decency, there were moments of grace and redemption. These moments usually came at the end of each episode, as Denny and Alan hung out on the balcony of their high-rise office and cemented their unique friendship. In one episode, Denny caught a glimpse of Alan hanging out on the balcony with another lawyer at the firm. Later, the following conversation took place between Denny and Alan:

DENNY: Don't talk to me.

ALAN: It's not like I went fishing with him.

DENNY: And don't make fun of me. I don't know whether you know this—not many men take the time every day to . . . talk to their best friend. That's not something most men have.

ALAN: No, it isn't.

DENNY: What I give to you, what—what I share, I do with no one else. I like to think what you give to me, you do with nobody else. Now that—that may sound silly to you. But here's what I think is silly—the idea that jealousy or fidelity is reserved for romance. I always suspected that there was a connection between you and THAT man. That you got something you didn't get from me.

ALAN: I probably do. But gosh, what I get from you, Denny . . . People walk around today calling everyone their "best friend." The term doesn't have any real meaning anymore. Mere acquaintances are lavished with hugs and kisses upon a second or, at most, third meeting. Birthday cards get passed around offices, so everybody can scribble a snippet of sentimentality for a colleague they've barely met. And everyone just "loves" everyone. As a result, when you tell somebody you love them today, it isn't much heard. I love you, Denny. YOU are my best friend. I can't imagine going through life without you as my best friend. Not gonna kiss you, however.

DENNY: I don't want you on my balcon . . . on ANY balcony, alone—with THAT man.

ALAN: Okay.[2]

We may assume that time spent with a person or shared experiences or even marriage automatically make people friends. This is not true. What makes someone a friend?

After three years of time with his disciples, Jesus said this to them: "I no longer call you servants. . . . Instead, I have called you friends" (John 15:15).

What happened? What changed in their relationship with him that Jesus now considered them to be friends? Two things occurred. First, he shared who he really was with them. And second, he sacrificed for them. These two things defined friendship for Jesus.

## SHARING WHO YOU ARE

Great marriages are grounded in great friendships, and great friends know each other. They spend time talking and listening. Friends open up their hearts to each other and share their hurts and hopes. A popular term for this is *intimacy*. It refers to a detailed knowledge or understanding of someone or something.

Marriage expert John Gottman calls this kind of knowledge of a person's inner world a "Love Map."[3] A love map is all the stored information you have about your partner's life. To be a great friend to your spouse means sharing who you really are, the good and the bad. It also means that you listen and learn about your spouse. You know them better than anyone else.

> Happy marriages are based on a deep friendship. . . . These couples tend to know each other intimately—they are well versed in each other's likes, dislikes, personality quirks, hopes, and dreams.
> —John Gottman

When did the disciples become Jesus' friends? Historians believe it started with an event in Jesus' life called the transfiguration. Recorded in Mark 9, Jesus took three of his followers up onto a mountain. There his appearance changed. His clothes became dazzling white. At that moment, his followers realized that he was more than a local Jewish rabbi; he was a divine being. Up until that point, who he was and what he was about had been hidden. There and from then on, Jesus began talking to his disciples about dying for the sins of the world. Friendship is when we remove the veil hiding who we are from everyone else, and we allow our friend to know us on a deeper level. It may happen on a mountaintop, on a balcony, or in a corner of Starbucks, but sharing who we really are (or knowing someone intimately) is not enough. But there is more to friendship than only allowing our friend to know us.

## SACRIFICING FOR EACH OTHER

Jesus said his friends love each other with a sacrificial love. Friendship means sacrificing our own desires, agendas, or needs for another person. It comes in a variety of forms:

- Doing an activity that your partner enjoys
- Going out of your way to do something kind for your partner
- Accepting your partner's quirks and imperfections
- Adjusting or cancelling your plans when your partner needs you
- Not forcing them to believe in everything the same way you do
- Having good manners in conversation (listening, not interrupting, keeping the focus on them)

Great friendships happen when we know another person intimately and sacrifice ourselves for his or her sake. Unhealthy friendships go the other way—when we make others sacrifice themselves for the needs of our inner world.

## NEED VS. LOVE

Janice was newly engaged but not happy. She and Anthony had been dating for three years and living together for six months. When he proposed, she thought the anger she felt toward him would change. It didn't.

"He can be really . . . controlling," she privately confessed.

"And you love him?" I asked.

"Yeah, I can't live without him."

"What does that mean?" I asked.

"It means 'I love him.'"

"I guess I'm asking do you love him or do you need him?"

She paused and responded with the following statement or question: "I guess . . . I need to love him?"

Love is not about filling a void we have; it's about allowing what we have to flow into the life of another person. Marriages veer off course and head toward destruction when couples begin to view their spouse as the person God intends to meet our needs. We are friends with our mate when we know and love them for who they are, not for what they can or cannot do for us.

> The beginning of love is to let those we love be perfectly themselves, and not to twist them to fit our own image. Otherwise we love only the reflection of ourselves we find in them.
> —Thomas Merton

## THREE STAGES OF RELATIONSHIPS

As human beings, we are designed to move through three stages in our relationship with others. The first stage is dependence. When we are young, we are dependent on others for our basic physical and emotional needs. As children, we not only have our food and security needs met by our family, but we also receive our self-concept and view of the world from them. As we move into our young adult years, the next stage begins—independence. In this stage, we are challenged to do things on our own. We are encouraged to set goals and achieve them. We are also allowed to suffer the consequences for poor choices and behavior. At this stage, we also become aware that our sense of self-worth and value must not be dependent on the views of others. The last stage is called interdependence. This is when, having received the security and guidance of the first stage and the motivation and self-confidence of the second stage, we are able to interact with others in a healthy way.

> Doom awaits any relationship where one person is trying to
> change the other into something or someone they aren't.
> —Les and Leslie Parrott

Many of us come to relationships having a less than ideal passage through these stages. Some are attracted to a potential mate because one or both of them is still working through some dependency stage issues. This was Janice's problem. She needed someone to change. She needed someone outside of herself to prove she was worth something. Even her seemingly loving desire to help him with his anger was self-serving. It helped her feel needed. It wasn't love, it was dependency.

The Broadway musical *Wicked* illustrates the sometimes self-serving dependency that masquerades as friendships. In the satirical spin on *The Wizard of Oz*, Glinda is a spoiled and narcissistic princess of the witch school (and future Good Witch of the North). Elphaba is a quiet, unattractive, and misunderstood girl from the other side of the tracks (and future Wicked Witch of the West).

Glinda: Elphie, now that we're friends, I've decided to make you my new project.

Elphaba: You really don't have to do that.

Glinda: I know. That's what makes me so nice!

Whenever I see someone less fortunate than I,

And let's face it, who isn't less fortunate than I?

My tender heart tends to start to bleed

And when someone needs a makeover

I simply have to take over!

I know I know exactly what they need!

And even in your case

Though it's the toughest case I've yet to face

Don't worry, I'm determined to succeed!

Follow my lead,

And yes, indeed, You will be . . .

Popular![4]

> I think the most important thing is not to try very hard [to make friends].
> The older you get, I think people get suspicious of people who
> are trying too hard to do anything.
> —Geoffrey Greif

The musical's hit song "Popular" comes from Glinda's discovery of Elphaba, who is simply a pawn in her self-serving dependency on others. True love is jeopardized when we have too much of our own needs riding on our relationship with another person. Too much independence, however, is also a threat.

Interdependence is when we come to the relationship as a whole person, but compromise and share with the other. An interdependent woman does not need her man, but wants him. She freely adjusts her life to include his. An interdependent man does not simply include his woman in his already completed life, but he allows her to make his life complete in a new and different way from his own. The Bible says, the two "will become one flesh" (Gen. 2:24). This does not mean that they are incomplete without the other; rather a new one-flesh union is formed from two whole people.

> Interdependence, a hallmark of friendship, means that your activities, plans, and decisions influence those of your friend and hers influence yours.
> —Florence Isaacs

## FRIENDSHIP IS TWO-WAY

I hate flimsy handshakes. If I shake someone's hand, I want an equal or greater handshake from him or her. A weak handshake says, "I'm doing this out of obligation. I'm not in this." Friendship is like a handshake. Each person has to give to it for it to be meaningful. Friendship love is two way. This is called reciprocity. It's when each person is giving to the relationship.

Some relationships feel like friendships, but they are not reciprocal. Counseling is a good example. You share your feelings and thoughts with a counselor. He or she provides support, direction, and feedback. You may see each other regularly. But it is not a friendship. The counselor does not say, "OK, my turn. Here's what I am struggling with." Ministry relationships are another example. When I was being trained as a hospital chaplain, my supervisor said, "When you visit people in the hospital, the visit is about them. Let them share, ask them how they are doing, and listen to their story." When providing ministry to someone, we are giving them charity (a Latin word for *agape*, the one-way unconditional love).

Friendship love is when we give to each other; we take turns. What do we take turns doing?

## PLAYING

Dr. Willard Harley of Marriage Builders encourages finding a way to make your spouse your "recreational companion."[5] Take up a sport or activity together. Physical activity and recreation create connections emotionally and physically that are not achieved any other way. Playing also keeps fun and enjoyment in the relationship. Playing may change over time, given schedules, family commitments, or health issues, but always looking for new ways to play is one way to keep friendship in marriage strong. Friends say, "Let's have some fun!"

## TALKING

Two-way communication is important in marriage. Friends talk to each other. They share their thoughts, dreams, fears, and questions with each other. Making time for talking is a challenge in our media-saturated culture. Turning off the television or radio, removing the ear buds, and maybe escaping to a nearby coffee shop regularly is how friendship is reinforced. Friends ask, "What's on your mind?"

> There are many kinds of talk, and the mere flow of words between two people does not guarantee intimacy. Nevertheless, there can be no intimacy *without* conversation. To know and love a friend over the years, you must have regular talks.
> —Alan Loy McGinnis

## FIGHTING

After Marie and I married, we avoided conflict at all costs. Seeing the damage it caused in our homes growing up, we went to the other extreme and avoided fighting. The results were disastrous: resentment, fears, and hurt feelings. About four years into our marriage, we said to each other, "Let's start fighting." We've been fighting ever since! We came up with simple rules for fair fighting. Friends don't avoid conflict; they trust each other enough to get through the conflict fairly. Friends say, "Let's work this out."

## PLANNING

I always encourage couples to have plans. What will they be doing this year? How will they grow closer to each other, God, and others? Plans give us a direction to go and keep us focused on getting there. Plans also have a way to keep us grounded in what we believe. Marriages are great when each person contributes to a shared plan—it could be short-term or long-term. Friends ask, "What do you want to do?"

## HELPING

Who does what in this marriage? How do we cooperate in doing life together? Employment, individual strengths, experience, and gender roles are involved when deciding how to share responsibilities. Many couples struggle because they feel like one is doing more than the other. To be a friend in marriage means that you graciously and honestly talk and resolve to share the burdens of life. Friends say, "Let me help you with that."

In each of these five areas, we show reciprocity—friendship that is two way. We both come to the relationship and meet each other in playing, talking, fighting, planning, and helping. These are not the responsibility of one, but both. Each person plays a part.

## SAME BUT DIFFERENT

Friendship love is two way, but not always in the same way. Being friends in marriage means that we are able to see, value, and share the unique strengths we each bring to the relationship.

In the 1980's classic movie, *The Karate Kid*, Mr. Miyagi, the wise Karate mentor, sees a picture of his young apprentice, Daniel, and Daniel's love interest. With a grunt of Buddhist simplicity he says, "Look good together . . . different, but same."[6]

> Friendships are not designed to be well-rounded; 83 percent of the people we have studied report that they bring different strengths to the relationship than their best friend does. This is why it's so damaging when another person focuses on what *we do not bring* to the friendship.
> —Tom Rath

Couples struggle when they assume that their spouse will give back what is given to them in the same way. One woman told me, "I am a really good listener, and I expect him to be too." Speaking of his wife, a friend told me, "I don't know why she's always so excited about things. Why can't she just chill out more . . . like me!"

Tom Rath calls this the "Rounding Error."[7] It is the belief that our spouse can be everything we want them to be—the best listener, helper, advice giver, sports fan, craft partner, or whatever we are looking for. Marriages are best when couples discover and enjoy the unique things their partners bring to the relationship. When we accept each other for the unique strengths we bring to the relationship, we protect our marriage from resentment and disappointment.

This allows us to not place such heavy demands on our spouse and helps us understand the importance of friendships outside the marriage.

## FRIENDS OUTSIDE OF MARRIAGE

In chapter 1, we talked about spousal idolatry, that is, putting your spouse before God. If this is the first deadly sin of marital love, the second is making your spouse your friend to the exclusion of all others. We need friends outside our marriage—both male and female.

> That is why those pathetic people who simply "want friends" can never make any. The very condition of having Friends is that we should want something else besides Friends.
> —C. S. Lewis

When Marie and I first married, everyone else took a back seat to our relationship. In fact, everything did. The beginning of a new union is a wonderfully blissful time; lovers often find themselves completely absorbed in each other. This is generally a good thing. Couples need time to bond and fully enjoy the newness of their relationship. The

Bible seems to encourage this as well. Jewish law prohibited a man from being involved in certain activities for the first year of marriage, so he could "stay at home and bring happiness to the wife he has married" (Deut. 24:5).

While the bonding of husband and wife is vitally important, maintaining, growing, and creating new friendships outside the marriage is vital to a strong marriage because our spouse should not be the center of the universe. Friendships are great when we want to talk about personal things, and our spouse may not be the right person to talk to about those particular things. They are also great when you want to talk about nothing! Mark Galli writes:

> To be sure, I want my wife to tell me when she's concerned about work or some relational debacle. I still want to understand and appreciate her interests. But now I don't expect to fully get it sometimes, and we both have other people in our lives who, in some areas, will get it.
>
> This means we also have the freedom not to know every single detail that's going on in each other's lives. There are some things I share with other guys that I won't share with Barb. There are some things she shares with other women that I don't need to know about."[8]

Having good friendships outside the marriage helps us come back to our spouse as a more whole and balanced person. Being a good friend in marriage means encouraging your spouse to have other good friends too.

## WHAT IS A GOOD FRIEND?

You may have a lot of friends or maybe only a few, but are they good friends? Some friendships are toxic—they are damaging to our sense of well-being and can even threaten our marriages. Having good friendships outside of marriage will be a blessing to the friendship inside our marriage.

> Friendship is based on shared values and goals. At a simple level, two people could be friends just because they both enjoy golf or crafts or gossip. Deeper friendship happens, however, when people share the deepest and most important values.
> —Carol Kent and Karen Lee-Thorp

*GOOD FRIENDS ARE LOYAL.* They support you and believe in you when the world attacks. They don't always agree with you, but they always believe the best about you. They stand by you when things are tough. They always want to hear your side of things and want to help you fulfill your dreams.

*GOOD FRIENDS ARE AVAILABLE.* They are on-call for you. They want to do things with you and ask you to do things with them. They share common interests with you and will usually build their schedule around yours. They get together with you regularly and look forward to seeing you again. They are always asking how they can help, how you have been, and what is new in your life.

*GOOD FRIENDS ARE VALUE PARTNERS*. They share your basic beliefs about God, relationships, and decision making. They may be very different than you, but at the core, they are kindred spirits. They encourage you to live what you believe and hold you accountable when your actions don't match what you hold to be true.

*GOOD FRIENDS ARE MARRIAGE FRIENDLY*. They want your marriage to work. They always ask you what kind of spouse you are being. They point you back to working on yourself and refuse to give in to complaint parties you try to have about your spouse. They hear your marital woes but are solution oriented. They also make sure your eyes are not looking outside your marriage.

## SAFE BOUNDARIES

I met with a couple recently that wanted to rebuild their relationship. I'll call them Dennis and Rachel, and they have been married for five years. Dennis is a successful salesman in a large pharmaceutical company. He is driven, articulate, and charismatic. Rachel works in the art world part time and is transitioning to being a stay-at-home mom. She is six months pregnant. She is intuitive, disciplined, and empathetic.

"Dennis is away twice a month, and I'm worried," Rachel said.

"You don't have to be worried. Nothing is going to happen," Dennis attempted to reassure her.

"Nothing like what?" I asked.

"OK . . . a few years ago, I went away on business, and I had dinner with a colleague."

"You kissed her," Rachel said.

"I hugged her at the end of the dinner. She gave me a peck on the cheek."

"Why?"

"I don't know. I think she liked me."

"Who else was at the dinner?" I asked.

"It was just us, but we work together all the time! I think Rachel is just insecure because she is pregnant," Dennis said.

"Dennis is a very attractive, very successful man. That is very appealing to women," Rachel reasoned. "And this has been a tough pregnancy on us. He works with a lot of strong, beautiful women, and there are a lot of single, party guys in his division."

"Rachel, your artist friends aren't exactly the picture of fidelity and godliness. The openings I've been at with you are just as bad as some nightclubs," Dennis countered.

> If you are married, you have an obligation to both God and your spouse to keep all your outside relationships from becoming sexualized.
> —Gregg Jantz

Dennis and Rachel have some strong emotions and insecurities, but clear and simple boundaries could help their marriage immediately. I spoke recently with a counselor friend of mine about her suggestions for protecting a relationship from temptation and infidelity. I compiled her thoughts and my own into four simple guidelines using the acronym SAFE.

## SPEAK ABOUT YOUR SPOUSE

If your spouse cannot be with you in person, make sure she is present in other ways. Talk about him in affirming ways when you can. Have her picture in your office. If God designs us to be one in marriage, then speak or act as if your spouse were there with you at all times. I was in a conversation with a woman the other day who seemed to be communicating interest and affection toward me. She mentioned a movie she'd seen recently. My reply was, "My wife and I saw that one the other night for our weekly movie night. We loved it." Well-placed "wes" are helpful for reinforcing to others (and ourselves) that we are not available for romantic interests.

## AVOID SOME THINGS

As a general rule, certain conversations should be off-limits. Never talk about marital problems with a member of the opposite sex. Sometimes people ask questions to try to understand their spouse, but the best person to ask about this is their spouse. Sexual topics should also be avoided. In addition to these conversations, time alone and inappropriate touching should be avoided. Steering clear of blatantly tempting situations is important as well (for example, marriage-hostile bachelor parties, limit-pushing office events, business trips with a lot of free time).

> Increasingly, modern-day affairs do not [necessarily] involve sex. . . . The best way to determine if you are becoming too close to your friend is to focus honestly on the amount of time you think about that friend. If you are married and invent excuses or unimportant reasons to see him or her, the alarm bells should be going off in your head. This isn't healthy.
> —Shmuley Boteach

## FEELINGS: KNOW THEM AND TALK ABOUT THEM

Statistics show that therapists and psychologists are less likely to cross boundaries and commit adultery than educators, politicians, and clergy.[9] Therapists and psychologists are trained to be aware of feelings going on inside them as they interact with others and are more likely to talk about the conflicting feelings they have. Confusion, shame, and embarrassment keep feelings secret, which leads to problems. Being able to know what you're feeling and have trusted people with whom to discuss things is essential for keeping safe boundaries.

## ENCOURAGE FRIENDSHIPS WITH SHARED VALUES

Florence Isaacs suggests having friendships that share the same views as you on issues like monogamy and commitment.[10] This includes having friendships with other married couples. The divorce rate is lower among couples who have mutual friends with shared values. When you get engaged, married, or are rebuilding a difficult marriage, you may have to reevaluate friendships to find those that can support you during these transitions.

When there has been infidelity in the relationship (or in a previous one), these SAFE guidelines may need to be ramped up to include no unmonitored conversations with the opposite sex (including e-mails, online social networking, etc.), having only married friends, and having only same-gender accountability partners for support and guidance.

## BEFRIENDING YOUR MATE

### GENDER MATTERS

Being friends with someone of the same gender may come more easily to us than befriending someone of the opposite gender. Consider the following generic differences between men and women:

| Men | Women |
|---|---|
| 1. Brain: Easy to Compartmentalize | 1. Brain: Easy to Integrate or Multitask |
| 2. Relational Style: Task or Decision Oriented | 2. Relational Style: People or Discussion Oriented |
| 3. Communication Style: Report | 3. Communication Style: Rapport |
| 4. Verbal Direction: Literal | 4. Verbal Direction: Indirect |
| 5. Decision Making: Solitary or Internal | 5. Decision Making: Communal or Verbal |
| 6. Risks: High Ability to Take Risks | 6. Risks: Cautious in Taking Risks |

Understanding how men and women work (especially in relation to marriage) is important in befriending your mate. Talk about and recognize the differences as they come up in daily life. And appreciate the gender-specific strengths your spouse has and how they add value to the relationship.

## DO THINGS TOGETHER

Couples need to find and maintain their common interests. Once a partnership is made, many couples invest time and energy in other things like working, schooling, volunteering, or raising children. Friendship is maintained by continuing to date each other.

> Unfortunately, many couples lose touch with one another as far as
> the simple pleasure of enjoying one another's company goes.
> Husband and wife, yes; friends, no. Over time they gradually drift apart.
> They forget the fun of experiencing life together. So, they build
> separate worlds that have little in common.
> —Robert Lewis and William Hendricks

Steve and Kristi decided to take up tennis. They played tennis all the time when they were dating and newly married, but over the years, their lives got busier. Playing tennis gave them time to rekindle their friendship apart from family, working, and other commitments of marriage.

## PROTECT YOUR PARTNER

When people have been together for a while, they are tempted to be less friendly to each other. They feel more open about sharing personal stories without permission. They may be less tolerant of mistakes or offenses. In the name of helping the other person grow, they are sometimes too blunt or rough.

Be careful about what you share about your spouse with others. Have you ever been with a couple and one of them says, "You know what she did the other day?" and a look of panic comes over the wife's face? Marie and I have a rule: Don't share unapproved stories. We have a bank of stories that are OK to share and discreet signals we give each other when an unapproved story starts to come out spontaneously.

Protect your spouse by not insulting or cutting him or her down in front of others. This is especially important for women to understand. Men are quickly emasculated in public settings by the simplest criticisms. The closer you are to a person, the more understanding and sensitive you need to be.

## APPRECIATE THE SEASONS

Marriages go through seasons. One season is life-giving, joyful, sexually fulfilling, and inspiring. Another season may be confusing, uneventful, or even lonely and painful. Great friendships know how to navigate through the seasons. They are not fair-weather friendships. One of the eight friendship roles identified by Tom Rath in his book, *Vital Friends*, is called a "Companion." I've found many couples who see their mate in this way:

> A Companion is always there for you, whatever the circumstances. You share a bond that is virtually unbreakable. When something big happens in your life—good or bad—this is one of the first people who calls. At times, a true Companion will even sense where you are headed—your thoughts, feelings, and actions—before you know it yourself. Companions take pride in your relationship, and they will sacrifice for your benefit. They are the friends for whom you might literally put your life on the line. If you are searching for a friendship that can last a lifetime, look no further than a Companion.[11]

We may have struggles (or losses) of faith when the spiritual brother or sister part of our relationship is challenged. When sexual intimacy takes a back seat at different stages in life, the lover side of our marriage will change. But our friendship can remain strong throughout the seasons of life.

## JOHN AND ABBIE'S STORY

One of the most notable friendships in American history is that of John and Abigail Adams. Before he became the second president of the United States, John was instrumental in helping draft the Declaration of Independence, while maintaining an inspiring and passionate partnership with his wife, Abigail, mostly through letters they exchanged during the founding of the country. Spanning over forty years and written across four hundred miles, the letters of John and Abigail Adams are an intimate picture of what makes a great marriage.

What was their secret?

### THEY DEEPLY RESPECTED EACH OTHER

Not only do their letters reflect the manners customary of their day, it is clear that John and Abigail cared what each other thought. John often asked Abigail her thoughts on important matters of state. Abigail, a woman ahead of her time, concerned herself not only with domestics matters like keeping the home and raising children, but also served as an advocate for women's rights and was John's eyes and ears back home. History records them as equals in helping with the original documents of America.

> Is there no way for two friendly souls to converse together, although the bodies are four hundred miles off? Yes, by letter. But I want a better communication. I want to hear you think or to see your thoughts. The conclusion of your letter makes my heart throb more than a cannonade would. You bid me burn your letters. But I must forget you first.
> —John Adams

## THEY WERE VERY PLAYFUL

Many of the letters are addressed to and signed in their pet names for each other, revealing that very personal and playful side couples have. John called her Miss Adorable, Nabby, and Diana (after the Greek goddess). Abigail would sometimes sign her letters Portia. Most often, their letters carried the lovingly simple moniker, My Dearest Friend. This playfulness enabled them to navigate back and forth between matters of state, home life, spiritual matters, and the deep romantic longing they had for each other. Their light-hearted teasing helped offset the challenges of a long-distance relationship.

## THEY EMPOWERED AND CHALLENGED EACH OTHER

They had a wise balance of tenderness and frankness in conflict. They disagreed on a variety of issues, women's rights being the most often noted. In Abigail's now famous letter to John, she emphasizes the importance of women's suffrage with the phrase "remember the ladies." His response, while deciding on a slower approach to women's rights, contains a sly acknowledgement that male privilege is "little more than a theory" anyway. Their writing shows their great ability to not allow conflict to sever their communication. In fact, their writing allowed them just the opposite, the freedom to say things they may have never said in person. Whether they agreed or disagreed, they shared their hearts and minds with each other, empowering and challenging each other to greatness.

> My pen is always freer than my tongue. I have written many things to you that I suppose I never could have talked.
> —Abigail Adams

## THEY SHARED A COMMON PASSION

They had a great vision—a country based on freedom and liberty. They were both willing to sacrifice many of the pleasures couples usually enjoy for the greater cause of a homeland free of tyranny. As the months wore on, they reassured themselves that their great assignment in helping form the union was worth the toll it took on their relationship, and they wrote all the more. Though they shared a common passion, they passionately reminded themselves of their love for one another.

> I must intreat you, my dear partner in all the joys and sorrows, prosperity and adversity of my life, to take a part with me in the struggle.
> —John Adams

He supported her in times of deep grief and loss. She supported him in handling his financial dealings. They gave each other words of encouragement from Scripture. They planned for their future together. They were partners in all areas of life and, most importantly, they considered themselves friends.

Two of the most influential people in the founding of the United States were a married couple. They found the strength and support within their relationship to transcend distance, trials, and political turmoil to not only change the country, but also forge a lasting friendship of love.

> . . . although I have a Number of Friends, and many Relations who are very dear to me, yet all the Friendship I have for others is far unequal to that which warms my heart for you.
> —John Adams

I am, and till then, and forever after will be your Admirer and Friend and Lover.

—Abigail[13]

*Jesus, my Friend,*

*You call us your friends. Help us to see the importance of friendship, in our marriage and outside of it. Through your love, empower us to become better friends to each other. In the good times and challenging times, may we learn to enjoy the affection, playfulness, and equality that come from being friends, and may we be great companions through all the seasons of marriage.*

*In Jesus' Name,*
*Amen*

## DISCUSSION STARTERS

1. What do you believe was most important in this chapter?
2. After reading this chapter, what (if anything) do you and your spouse have different beliefs about? In what areas are your beliefs and values about friendship similar?
3. What do you believe is the most important attribute of friendship?
4. What unique differences do you bring to your relationship? In what ways do those differences help the relationship?
5. In what ways can you improve the *philia* love with your spouse? Be very specific.

## LOVE IN ACTION

1. Read the following Scriptures about friendship and write down what you see as the big idea of the passage. Discuss with your spouse how these Scriptures relate to your friendship with each other and others: Proverbs 11:13; 12:26; 17:17; and 27:17.

2. Make a list of the top four boundaries you have in place to protect you from inappropriate behavior with friends of the opposite sex. If you do not have any such boundaries, think of at least two ways to protect your relationship from temptation. Discuss these with your partner.

3. Read *Vital Friends* by Tom Rath. Go online and create a vital friend profile for your spouse and two close friends. Plan and create three new ways you can play to the strengths of your friends to improve your relationships with them.

4. Write a letter to your spouse. Choose a nice card or stationery for the letter. Express your feelings and thoughts about your partner. Mention specific things that you appreciate about him or her. Don't use the letter as a confessional or to try convincing your partner to do something. Close your letter with a sincere desire to grow in your relationship. Leave the letter for him or her in a special place.

## RECOMMENDED READING

*The Relationship Cure: A 5 Step Guide to Strengthening Your Marriage, Family, and Friendships* by John Gottman

*Relationships* by Les and Leslie Parrott

*Rocking the Roles: Building a Win-Win Marriage* by Robert Lewis and William D. Hendricks

*Vital Friends: The People You Can't Afford to Live Without* by Tom Rath

# LOVERS

I think I could fall madly in bed with you.
—author unknown

*eros* [eer-os]: physical love; sexual yearning
or desire; sexual drive; libido.

> Eat, O friends, and drink; drink your fill, O lovers.
> —Song of Songs 5:1

Marie and I referred to it as chapter 9. It was the Sexual Relationship section of the workbook we completed before marrying.[1] There was a list of activities for us both to review and note if we would do them with the other or not:

- Take a shower and bath together.
- Engage in oral sex.
- Write something sexually provocative.
- Help reach orgasm.
- Wear sexually stimulating clothing.
- Present myself to you in the nude.

Marie and I couldn't wait to read each other's answers (and add some more to the ones listed). We waited to cover chapter 9 until the end of our engagement. As Christians, we were working hard to maintain our sexual purity. We believed that sex was a gift from God to be opened at the proper time, like a Christmas present. We were like children waiting to tear open the package!

The young man and woman of Song of Songs refer to themselves as brother and sister and friends, but the term of affection used most often is *lover*. Sensual and erotic love in marriage is the theme of this ancient poem. The woman says, "I am my lover's and my lover is mine" (Song 6:3).

*Eros* is the Greek word for sexual love. It is the physical yearning that draws a person to someone else. It is the love expressed in sensual pleasure—smell, taste, and touch. In marriage, it is the culmination of the first two relationships with our spouse—brother or sister and friend. *Eros* is intended to be fully and passionately embraced when two people have committed themselves in lifelong trust to one another.

## SEXPECTATIONS

When did you learn about sex? What did you learn? How important is sex? Consider the following quotes from Hugh Hefner and Larry Flynt, two of the most notorious pornographers of the twentieth century: "The major civilizing force in the world is not religion, it is sex"[2] and "Relax, it's only sex."[3]

According to these men who have made billions on the subject, either sex is more important than faith, or sex is something we should aggressively enjoy and not worry so much about. For a culture so drenched in sexuality, we should have this subject mastered. The statistics paint a disheartening picture:

- Experts speculate up to 10 percent of the total Christian population in the U.S. is sexually addicted.[4]
- One in six women (and one in thirty-three men) will be sexually assaulted in their lifetime.[5]
- Fifty percent of those married and over 60 percent of those unmarried experience sexual dissatisfaction.[6]
- Over 90 percent of men and women have negative sexual experiences in their past.[7]
- The rate of sexual dysfunction is higher for women.[8]

Our current situation is the result of two failures: a failure of education and a failure of integration. What we learn about sex and sexuality is often so removed from spirituality that it is harmful. In addition to this, sexuality is separated from a larger experience of life and relationships, so we are more selfish and disconnected than ever.

Wherever and whatever we have learned about sex, most of us come to marriage with certain myths in our minds. Here are a few common ones.

MYTH 1: IF WE ARE REALLY IN LOVE, GREAT SEX WILL JUST HAPPEN

While God designed us to be able to have sex with very little instruction, fulfilling and satisfying sex is not the direct result of being in love. Too many couples rely on passion and excitement rather than learning and commitment for a happy sex life.

> True passion and great sex don't just happen, but we can make great sex happen in our marriages by being deliberate about what we know works.
> —Clifford and Joyce Penner

I began my doctorate program under the instruction of a great preacher. Gathered together with other pastors and teachers, we were ready to have our preaching gifts affirmed and further our education.

"You are not great preachers," he said.

*What?* I thought. *He doesn't know me! How can he say that?*

He continued, "I know your congregations love you, and you preach with passion and enthusiasm. They are enthralled because you are new and exciting. In five years, if you have not learned to preach and understand yourself more, you will lose their interest, and they will simply tolerate you because you are committed to them. I want you to learn how to be great preachers, so you can give them the best for a long time."

In a similar way, great lovers are not born; they are grown. Sex may be great in the beginning, but that is because it is new. This is one reason one-night stands are so damaging. If they are sexually satisfying, they create a false norm to which marital sex will be compared. The feeling of being in love can start things off well, but great sex happens as each person commits to learning and growing to understand themselves and their spouse over a lifetime.

## MYTH 2: I SHOULD BE A GREAT LOVER FROM THE BEGINNING

David was not concerned about his wedding night. Sex was not new to him. He didn't consider himself a player, but he'd had enough sexual experiences to believe he could satisfy his new bride, especially since she was a virgin. Sharon did not come to the wedding night as confident. She was intimidated. She felt pressure to live up to those other women, and she secretly resented that she'd saved herself for David, but he'd slept with others. Their wedding night was not satisfying for either of them. David was frustrated that all the things that worked with the other women didn't work with Sharon. And Sharon felt like she was getting worked.

The most important factor in having a fulfilling sex life is to know your spouse, and an intimate knowledge of him or her does not come from an intimate knowledge of other partners (or from books). The Bible encourages men: "dwell with [your wife] according to knowledge" (1 Pet. 3:7 KJV). This rather wooden translation contains a much deeper meaning. The phrase "dwell with" suggests sexual intimacy and relationship, not just living arrangements. The best intimate relations come from an intimate knowledge of the person. I tell couples, "Have fun, learn, talk, try things, and give yourselves time to get to know each other."

> Isn't it enough that we all must constantly prove ourselves and compete in the marketplace, in the classroom, and in life in general outside the home? Life is full of competition whereby our standing as human beings, our potential for productivity, and our utility to those around us is constantly called into question and rated. What we need, amid this background of constantly proving ourselves, is a place where we can retire from the incessant pressure of everyday life, and into the arms of someone who loves us and wants to be with us just for what we are, rather than how we can be used.
> —Shmuley Boteach

Rasheed and Cori had the pleasure of starting fresh. Their traditional Middle Eastern upbringing helped them stay sexually pure while their friendship developed into a romance. I asked them for their thoughts on how their relationship developed from brother and sister in Christ to friends to lovers. Cori wrote:

The spiritual/friendship part for sure relates to the lover part! Without these, we wouldn't be true lovers! Having that bond of brotherhood/sisterhood/friendship helps us to be with one another physically in a more real way. As you know, we have saved ourselves for each other and this (in spite of our lack of sexual skills, though we're working on it!) has been such a blessing. We feel loved by one another, comfortable, and have fun. We trust each other and joke around, and this helps a lot. Being lovers is easy because we have the commitment that we are only with each other. We want to satisfy each other's needs and feel truly connected to one another.[9]

## MYTH 3: MEN ARE RESPONSIBLE FOR SEX IN THE RELATIONSHIP

While some couples will feel most comfortable with a more traditional sexual style (man initiates, woman responds), this understanding of sex is fraught with misunderstandings. Contemporary and ancient wisdom encourages a man to adapt his sexual activity to the rhythms and patterns of his wife. Men, biologically and emotionally, are almost always available and interested in sex. If men are encouraged to initiate based on their natural desire, their poor wives will find themselves saying no more than yes. In addition to having a more active libido, men connect sexuality with emotional well-being. If the sex is good, life is good. Men feel more loved and accepted when their wives are sexually responsive to them. Despite what many women believe, there is a lot going on in the male brain during sex. The release of the chemical oxytocin during orgasm serves as a pain reliever and relaxant in men. It is much like the response when the same chemical is released in babies during breastfeeding—it soothes the baby to comfort and sleep.

> Being proactive—working with your husband to build a fulfilling physical relationship—is so healthy for your husband's spiritual standing. At times, this will be a joy for you; at other times, it may feel like work, or even a dreaded chore. But on every occasion, I hope you see it as an expression of concern for your husband's spiritual well-being.
> —Gary Thomas

Female sexuality is more cyclical and rhythmic. Given a woman's menstrual cycle and hormonal patterns, generally speaking, a woman's body naturally provides for sexual time together and time apart. Sexual intercourse is countered by a time of menstruation (during which most women prefer not to be intimate) allowing for non-sexualized relationship building. But if a couple's sexual life is centered in her sexuality, she must understand herself.

For most women, desire comes before arousal. This is different for men who often experience desire and arousal at the same time (and may even confuse the two). Women are encouraged to experiment and enjoy their sexuality in marriage by responding and initiating sex when they sense the desire for intimacy, knowing that arousal will follow later.

Couples should take turns initiating or be clear about the signs that their partner is interested and aroused. Men should place the pleasure and enjoyment of their wives above their own, and women should make loving choices to initiate sex, respond whole-heartedly to initiation, or communicate love when sex is not possible. Both people are responsible for creating and growing sexual love in the relationship.

## MYTH 4: IF IT WILL ENHANCE THE PLEASURE, IT'S GOOD

Many good marriages have been destroyed in the name of enhancing sexual pleasure. Pornography is a good example of how this myth plays out. The use of pornography by couples is increasing rapidly. While the research shows that the use of pornography can increase sexual interest and frequency within a relationship, its effects on a couple's intimacy can be disastrous.[10] Pornography is like a drug in that, with some people, the need for more becomes obsessive. It also has a way of discouraging the closeness the couple had been hoping it would foster.

> Eros, honoured without reservation and obeyed
> unconditionally, becomes a demon.
> —C. S. Lewis

The Christian ministry, XXXchurch.com, features regular articles and interviews from those who have left the adult entertainment industry. Their stories of loneliness, abuse, and sexual dysfunction reinforce the reality that the desire to increase pleasure and sexual fulfillment through pornography ends in heartbreak—something professionals in sexual therapy have known for years.

If *eros* is not fundamentally self-centered, since it has to do with a strong desire within us to experience something sexually powerful, it is the kind of love most vulnerable to misuse and abuse. If we give into it without regard, we will harm ourselves and others. *Eros* must have limits. I've heard this stated in different ways over the years: "The erotic fire should be as big and powerful as possible, as long as it stays in the fireplace" or, "The strong waves of the river of passion bring life, but once they have escaped the banks they bring death."

This echoes the wisdom of Hebrews 13:4: "Marriage should be honored by all, and the marriage bed be kept pure, for God will judge the adulterer and sexually immoral." The God of creation created sexuality. Creativity and variety is healthy in a marriage relationship, but there are things that can hurt the relationship. Sexuality was made to be enjoyed fully but within certain boundaries. Sexual love is best experienced when we consider God's design and guidelines.

## MYTH 5: I WILL ONLY BE SEXUALLY ATTRACTED TO MY SPOUSE

After our marriage suffered its devastating blow, Marie and I made a commitment: We would tell each other when we develop a crush on someone. Based on our relationship as spiritual siblings and friends, we recognized that feelings happen. It's what we do with our feelings that matter. For us, nothing extinguishes random inappropriate feelings of attraction to others like honesty with each other.

> The strongest sexual attraction may exist between persons so incompatible in tastes and capacities that they could not endure living together for a week much less a lifetime.
> —George Bernard Shaw

Some couples naïvely believe that God would never allow sexual feelings to arise in them for someone they are not totally committed to in marriage. Marriage does not magically protect us from sexual infidelity; *agape* and *philia* do. When we are committed to a spiritual union with God and our spouse and nurture our marriage friendship, we can extinguish the flames of *eros* when they threaten to harm us.

This myth is at the center of why many relationships fail. While some do not adequately protect their relationship from sexual temptation, others mistake sexual attraction with being in love and find themselves in a marriage with the absolutely wrong person for them.

## SEX DOES NOT EQUAL LOVE

Sex creates a powerful bond between two people. Even when sex is shallow and impersonal, something happens on a spiritual level that we don't quite understand. When sex is part of a committed relationship, that spiritual connection helps reinforce the love, trust, and acceptance each person feels. When there is not a committed relationship, it creates feelings of being used, cheap, or guilty. Insecurity and questions about one's acceptance arise. These are all signs that something meaningful to us has occurred and been misused.

> There's more to sex than mere skin on skin. Sex is as much spiritual mystery as physical fact. As written in Scripture, "The two become one." Since we want to become spiritually one with the Master, we must not pursue the kind of sex that avoids commitment and intimacy, leaving us more lonely than ever—the kind of sex that can never "become one."
> —1 Corinthians 6:16–17 MSG

Even if we only consider ourselves as physical or non-spiritual beings, our bodies reinforce that sex connects people in deep and meaningful ways. Oxytocin, the chemical mentioned in relationship to orgasm, is popularly called the cuddle drug. For women, oxytocin acts as a bonding agent. Oxytocin is the chemical related to attachment. This is why women can find themselves attached to the wrong kind of men when sex is introduced into the relationship without a faithful commitment of their male partner.

Dr. Judith Sills, in *Women's Encyclopedia of Health & Emotional Healing*, explains the consequences of this chemical bond:

> When you put sex early in a relationship, you make courtship and dating a much more vulnerable process. Most women tell me that they become emotionally attached when they take a lover. Emotional attachment makes you vulnerable . . . and because sex doesn't give men an automatic emotional attachment . . . It may come as a shock when she finds out the bond is not shared.[11]

> It's possible to be married to somebody and sharing the same bed and even having sex regularly and still be profoundly disconnected.
> —Rob Bell

Sex connects us in powerful ways. But let's not confuse it with love. Sex can create the feelings of relationship, even when relationship is absent. This is why premarital sex can lead couples to perceive that they are more compatible than they really are. Sex also creates the illusion that a marriage is OK when it is actually in need of great repair. The chemicals released in the body during sex send two messages. To the man, they say, "I'm alright; I can relax." To the woman, they say, "I mean something to him."

If the couple is in a committed marriage working to strengthen their relationship as spiritual siblings and friends, these messages are life-giving. If the relationship is not committed and the couple is simply enjoying their bodies, these messages are, at best, deceptive and, at worst, dangerous.

## ARE WE SEXUALLY COMPATIBLE?

"We might be spiritually compatible and have a good friendship, but are we sexually compatible?" What is this question really asking?

Do we have the same interest in sex?

Can he satisfy me?

Does she know what she is doing?

Are there physical problems that make sex unenjoyable?

What about personal issues that hinder sexuality?

Sexual compatibility is sometimes code-speak for "let's have sex and see if we enjoy it." There are better ways of assessing sexual compatibility than simply having sex since having sex is not a good measure of having a fulfilling, married sex life. How do we answer the questions above?

## THE NECESSITY OF ATTRACTION

I thought she was amazing. Petite, great legs, dark hair, exotic features. I thought I had the essential element of sexual compatibility: attraction. In a way, I was right. It happens differently for men and women. My attraction to Marie was immediate, as it is with most men who are visually oriented. Marie's attraction to me came later as she got to know me as a person. This is typical of women who find physical or sexual attraction secondary to other features of a man.

> When my date takes me home and kisses me good night, if I don't hear the philharmonic in my head, I dump him.
> —Barbara Streisand as Rose Morgan

Attraction—the spark that makes you feel alive around a person is important. When it is there, it's exciting but should not be confused with the makings of a great relationship. In addition to other forms of attraction, research shows that kissing is a good measurement of attraction.[12] When attraction is not there, you need to pay attention.

Ellie had been dating Troy for over a year. They attended church together, enjoyed activities together, and loved each other's families. Troy was well built, cute, and had a great personality, but there was one problem . . . Ellie felt no spark. It wasn't until they began talking about engagement that she was able to come out with it. She had tried to tell herself that those feelings would come. "He's a great candidate for marriage. He's got everything going for him! Am I being too superficial?" She knew she wasn't. She knew that if the attraction wasn't there, sexual compatibility would be a problem.

## TESTING THE SEX

"Don't we need to have sex to be sure we'll be sexually compatible?" Many dating or engaged couples feel the need to try it out, thinking there might be problems they need to know about before marriage. But many sexual problems are based in relationship issues (communication, conflicts, guilt or shame, selfishness), not physical issues. Here is a conversation I had with an engaged man recently:

"I think it's good to know if there are any physical problems before we go further," Joe said.

"What do you mean?" I asked.

"You know, sexual problems that would hinder the relationship."

"What if there are sexual problems that are physical?"

"What do you mean?" Joe asked.

"I mean, would you not get married?"

"Well, it depends what's going on."

"The sexual part of your marriage is so important, that you would be willing to break off the marriage?" I asked.

"I don't know," he admitted.

"What happens if the physical sexual problem comes up ten years into the marriage?"

"Well, then we are stuck."

> Your relationship helps you know if you can make your sex life work, not the other way around.

Sexuality has become a litmus test for many people. If the sex is great, then the relationship will be great. If the sex is not great, the relationship is doomed. We need to re-prioritize the love in our relationships. *Eros* does not make a relationship healthy. *Agape* and *philia* make a relationship healthy. If we want to have a fulfilling physical relationship, we need to begin with a selfless and loving relationship with the one we consider our friend.

LIVING TOGETHER

Another way dating and engaged couples attempt to assess their sexual compatibility is by living together. This is perhaps the worst thing for a potential marriage commitment. Research shows that cohabitation is more likely to result in breakup or divorce than a lifelong committed marriage.

Mike and Harriet McManus, in *Living Together: Myths, Risks & Answers*, explore the rather counterintuitive facts:

> But living together sets up a relationship for failure. It's a trap. The only question, in most cases, is whether the relationship will fail before or after the wedding.
>
> Studies show that half of cohabiting relationships end within fifteen months—without a wedding . . . one could argue, nearly half of cohabitations do result in marriage. But such couples face much greater odds of divorce—67 percent as opposed to the usual 45 percent for first marriages.[13]

What is the reason for this? There seem to be certain characteristics shared by those who choose cohabitation that work against what is essential to creating a strong, vibrant marriage.

*CONVENIENCE*. Many couples who choose to live together say they are doing it because it is easier (usually either money or ability to have sex more often is underneath this). With convenience as a primary value to the couple, a future marriage begins on unstable ground. Cohabitating couples tend to focus on the few things they agree on for living together rather than trying to improve the relationship as a whole.

> One advantage of marriage, it seems to me, is that when you fall out of love with [each other], it keeps you together until maybe you fall in love again.
> —Judith Viorst

*COMMITMENT.* Cohabitating couples tend to be hesitant about commitment. They believe living together is a commitment, but usually stop short of many things that show sacrificial commitment to a partner (such as sharing bank accounts or placing your partner on your life insurance). Couples who live together tend to avoid conversation about marriage and commitment.

When it comes to marriage, the danger of premarital sex and cohabitation is somewhat counterintuitive. How can you improve your likelihood of a great marriage? Don't have sex or live together until you are married.

## DEALING WITH SEXUAL REPAIR

Another important variable in sexual compatibility is our level of sexual brokenness. Joshua had struggled to overcome a compulsive habit of viewing pornography and masturbating which started when he was very young. A child of a single parent who worked full-time and with no siblings, Joshua was lonely much of the time. He was shy and kept to himself. The day before his eleventh birthday, he found a stash of pornographic magazines in a nearby dumpster. The images of women being sexually used and satisfied awakened his newly budding sexual feelings, and the masturbation soothed some of his loneliness and feelings of rejection. But inside, he felt guilty and embarrassed, so he quickly formed a pattern of retreating, viewing, masturbating, and then destroying the porn. The cycle continued until his engagement to Allie.

> When we don't identify the true problems in our lives, we cannot find lasting healing—and when we cannot find lasting healing, we feel lonely, frustrated, angry, and anxious. People cannot find lasting contentment when they seek false solutions to misidentified problems.
> —Mark and Debra Laaser

Joshua was very excited to marry Allie. She was fun, smart, and caring. She was also very excited about starting the sexual part of their relationship. "I'm so glad I'm getting married," he told his close friend. "I'm not going to have those problems anymore because I'll have Allie." He was wrong. It only took six months. After an argument, Joshua spent the night in a different room. He felt confused, lonely, and rejected. Like a messenger of the gods, pornography came to his mind. The next day started a year-long downward spiral into magazines, videos, and strip clubs. Joshua was struggling with sexual addiction stemming from deeper desires for affirmation and acceptance.

Sexual compatibility is complicated when one or both people in the relationship have not honestly and healthily dealt with their sexual brokenness. This was the case with Marie and me. Naïve and hopeful that our marriage would heal the wounded areas within ourselves, we stepped forward in faith without realistic discussion and help.

Consider Christine's story. Raised in a very traditional, strict, home, she had high expectations of herself. Her family pressured her to be an excellent student and model of Christian purity. When she was molested by a neighbor at five years old, she did everything she could to keep it a secret and worked hard to maintain her perfect image. As she moved into middle school, her parents became more restrictive, fearing she would make bad decisions. Christine silently struggled with the consequences of her abuse and found herself wanting the attention the boys at school gave her because of her developing figure. Christine had two secret boyfriends in high school. Both took advantage of her desire for attention—one used sex as a way to keep her, the other date-raped her.

> Intimacy once fused with abuse surfaces, to some degree or another, whenever intimacy is experienced in other relationships.
> —Dan Allender

When she met Anthony, she believed things would be different. He was a Christian. He cared about her. She found him attractive, and when she told him what she'd gone through, he didn't see her as damaged goods. They dated for four years, had a beautiful wedding ceremony, and began a new life together. Two years later, she found herself flirting with a coworker. She didn't understand what was happening with her. Sex with Anthony was good but not arousing. He wanted to try new things, and she was pulling away. She loved him, but part of her resented him. Though committed to marriage, she inwardly wanted the excitement of a new man. Christine was dealing with a common problem in women who have been sexually abused.[14] In Christine, a deep association was made between sexual arousal and abusive behavior. Normal, affirming, consensual sex seemed boring. The more wrong it felt, the more attracted she was. It was not long before an adulterous relationship began.

When couples say they are no longer in love or the spark is gone, it sometimes has to do with one of these problems. But God is bigger than sex. Whether our brokenness comes from our growing up years or from previous relationships, addiction, abuse, ambivalence, and even adultery can be repaired. Sexual incompatibility due to brokenness may be the end of a relationship founded on *eros*, but it does not need to be the end of a marriage grounded in *agape*. There is hope and healing, and we can find the sexual compatibility God longs for married couples to have.

> Sexual incompatibility due to brokenness may be the end of
> a relationship founded on *eros*, but does not need to be
> the end of a marriage grounded in *agape*.

## LET'S GET NAKED!

In an episode of the television show *Seinfeld* (1990–1998), Jerry Seinfeld's new girlfriend, Melissa, enjoys being naked most of the time. Jerry, who is eccentric and a germophobe, shares the details with his sex-deprived friend George.

GEORGE: She ate breakfast naked?

JERRY: She didn't even want a napkin.

GEORGE: I've had bedroom naked, I've had walk-to-the-bathroom naked . . . I have never had living-room naked.

JERRY: Oh, it's a scene.

GEORGE: It's like you're livin' in the Playboy Mansion! Did she, uh, did she frolic?

JERRY: I don't really have enough room.

Later, Jerry shows his disgust remembering his girlfriend's naked cough.

JERRY: Coughing . . . naked . . . It's a turn-off, man.

GEORGE: Everything goes with naked.

JERRY: When you cough, there are thousands of unseen muscles that suddenly spring into action. It's like watching that fat guy catch a cannonball in his stomach in slow motion.

GEORGE: Oh, you spoiled, spoiled man. Do you know how much mental energy I expend just trying to picture women naked?

JERRY: But the thing you don't realize is that there's good naked and bad naked. Naked hair brushing, good; naked crouching, bad.[15]

Agreeing to wear clothing all the time, Jerry and his girlfriend are unable to carry on a conversation without imagining one another naked. Jerry fantasizes about Melissa's beautiful body, and Melissa can only picture Jerry as a hairy Neanderthal. In the end, Jerry and his girlfriend break up.

## GOOD NAKED, BAD NAKED

The book of Genesis begins with the creation of the universe, the animal kingdom, and humanity. The man and woman, together representing God's image on earth, are brought together in the paradise of Eden as a couple. With simple elegance, Genesis 2:25 reads: "The man and his wife were both naked, and they felt no shame."

This is good naked.

Scholars do not believe this verse is included to romanticize nudity but rather to prepare the reader for the narrative that follows. Adam and Eve were presented with a choice—trust and fidelity to a God that loves them, or mistrust and self-motivated pleasure. As if archetypes of ourselves, they make the wrong choice. After cooperating together against God, Genesis 3:7–8 reads: "Then the eyes of both of them were opened, and they realized they were naked; so they sewed fig leaves together and made coverings for themselves . . . and they hid from the LORD."

This is bad naked.

Good naked is when we feel safe, accepted, and desired. Bad naked is when we feel insecure, compared, and rejected. The Hebrew word for naked is *arom*. It doesn't simply mean "without clothes." Its Greek equivalent in the New Testament means to be exposed or laid bare.[16] Both words imply a sense of vulnerability before God and God's law: "Nothing in all creation is hidden from God's sight. Everything is *uncovered* and *laid bare* before the eyes of him to whom we must give account" (Heb. 4:13, emphasis added).

Realizing the vulnerability, great lovers honor each other's nakedness. They affirm each other's bodies. They accept each other as is. They make each other feel safe. Good naked happens when we verbally affirm our spouse about who they are and how they look. It happens as we accept our bodies, as well as the gift God has given us. Good naked is about speaking to each other's unspoken sexual concerns and helping them feel loved.

> In the course of a marriage, both husbands and wives will face insecurity
> issues about their bodies. God desires for our mate to cheer us on, help
> us embrace his view of our bodies rather than the world's view.
> —Joseph and Linda Dillow

## NAKING

Being naked starts while our clothes are still on. A man kisses a woman for the first time. He hopes she will feel something special. A woman says, "I love you." She hopes he will respond with the same words. Before our flesh is exposed, we are naked. We take baby steps of trust and faith. C. S. Lewis called this "naking."[17] Like peeling away the layers of protection, we become more and more vulnerable.

In *Relationships*, Drs. Les and Leslie Parrot offer ten stages of intimacy that couples share:

1. Embracing and hand holding
2. Cuddling and gentle caressing
3. Polite kissing on the lips
4. Passionate total mouth kissing
5. Intense and prolonged mouth kissing
6. Fondling breasts and genitals outside the clothes
7. Fondling breasts and genitals under the clothes
8. Oral and genital stimulation to orgasm outside the clothes

9. Oral and genital stimulation to orgasm under the clothes
10. Genital intercourse[18]

The more vulnerable or "naked" we are, the more trust and commitment is needed. Shame appears when our nakedness is betrayed. Shame is the desire to cover, protect, and hide ourselves.

Naking is progressive. God's plan is for stages of commitment to accompany stages of intimacy—the more commitment and trust, the more nakedness. Couples have different ways of measuring this. Many dating and engaged couples I talk to find the tipping point around number five listed above. The momentum to be more intimate increases at this point. If a firm commitment and trust (like marriage) is not made, shame will probably result. During his engagement, one of my friends had a more simple measurement: "Don't touch anywhere fun."

Married couples looking to enhance their sexual relationship often find that numbers one to three have been neglected in their busy lives. Their naking may need to go in reverse.

## HAVING A GREAT THREESOME

Alex and Kadisha looked at each other and blushed. It wasn't the first time they'd had a great evening of lovemaking, but that night was extra special. They had returned from a weekend couples retreat their church hosted. During one of the sessions, they were instructed to talk through some of the challenges they had faced in their relationship. "Where was God during those times?" the facilitator asked.

> Two distinct persons; equal in value; with bone-deep emotional, spiritual, physical relatedness; totally transparent; without fear of being known. It is that kind of openness, acceptance, trust, and excitement to which we allude when we use the word *intimacy*.
> —Gary Chapman

They looked around the room at all the other couples who did not seem to know where to begin. They did. They took turns telling their story to each other. Alex talked about praying for the right woman in his life. Kadisha talked about meeting Alex when her father was deathly ill. Alex shared about having a mentor couple from church during their engagement. Kadisha remembered saying her vows and thinking, "I'm marrying my best friend." Alex talked about praying when they lost the baby. Kadisha mentioned the fear when Alex lost his job. The facilitator called time, but they weren't finished. They gave each other a knowing glance. On the drive home from the conference, Alex pulled over.

"Kadisha, I love you. Every day, when I wake up, I have this thing I do. I put my hand on your forehead, and I ask God to find ways to let you know how loved you are. I thank God for our marriage, our jobs, our honesty, your awesome body . . . everything."

That night was good naked and great lovemaking. Sex is simply another form of communication. Alex and Kadisha work hard to communicate—they listen, talk openly, trust each other, and do their best to understand and accept each other. They also have something else. They believe that God is the third party in all their conversations. When they think about their lives, God is there. They don't always know in what ways, but their relationship is a threesome—husband, wife, and God. This includes their sex life.

> Most couples don't see God as having any connection to their sexual lives. . . . If we leave God out of the bedroom, we will never taste the full pleasure and meaning of sex.
> —David Clarke

What does it look like to include God in your sex life? Here are a few ideas from Christian sex therapists Clifford and Joyce Penner:

- Thank God for the gift of sex and physical pleasure—some people are not as grateful as they should be. Maybe negative experiences have tainted your view of sex. Religious people are especially prone to having negative views of sex. Thank God, (explicitly) for the gift of sex.

- If you are married, do a Bible study with your spouse about sex. There are many good books and studies on the subject that are detailed but not inappropriately explicit.
- Pray about how you can be more pleasing to your spouse (in and out of the bedroom). Ask God to help you identify areas of selfishness, sin, fear, or unresolved sexual issues in your life.
- As a couple, spend time weekly praying about your intimacy. Of the ten stages listed previously, which are enjoyable, and which would you like to experience more? [19]

## SEX: THE MARRIAGE MEAL

In Song of Songs, the sexual experience is beautifully described through metaphors of agriculture. The husband describes his bride as a locked up garden and a fountain ready to explode (4:12). The woman's most intimate parts are referred to as a fragrant garden of "choice fruits" (see 4:13–15), and she invites her lover into the garden to taste and enjoy. Sex in marriage is like the sensual enjoyment of a delicious meal. To be fully satisfied with a sensuous meal, I recommend the following guidelines.

### EAT REGULARLY

Make time for sex. When committed to having sex regularly, you guard against "deprive and gorge" syndrome. Deprive and gorge is when your sex life rests on two extremes. On the one extreme, you are too busy, stressed, or tired to be available to your spouse. You also have unrealistic plans about when sex will find a place in the relationship. The other extreme is that, not knowing when sex will happen again, you have intense, quick, infrequent (and perhaps unsatisfying) sex. Sex in marriage should be both scheduled and spontaneous.

> Marge, there's just too much pressure. What with my job, the kids, traffic snarls, political strife at home and abroad. But I promise you, the second all those things go away, we'll have sex.
> —Homer Simpson

## EAT HEALTHY

Marie and I like to eat out a lot. When the food is good, we walk away feeling refreshed and strong. When the food is unhealthy, we feel weighed down and yucky. Sex is like that. God designed us to feel spiritually satisfied with obedience and to feel dirty (in a bad way) when we are in sin. This doesn't mean being boring. Variety is great. New positions, locations, and pleasures should be sampled, but caution should also be taken when considering things that will offend God or your spouse. What unhealthy or sinful things have made their way into your sex life? Maybe they had been attempts to spice things up, but now they are just burning your intimacy and trust.

## EAT IN CONSIDERATION OF THE OTHER

Nothing ruins a meal like one person selfishly finishing before the other. Sex is like a meal both people serve to each other, though sometimes sex is more geared toward one person than the other. Maybe he sometimes wants a quickie. She may sometimes enjoy receiving oral sex with no intercourse. "Considering one another" means we can mutually agree on how we can serve the other person and enjoy doing it.

> The marriage bed must be a place of mutuality—the husband seeking to satisfy his wife, the wife seeking to satisfy her husband. Marriage is not a place to "stand up for your rights." Marriage is a decision to serve the other, whether in bed or out.
> —1 Corinthians 7:3–4 MSG

## EAT, BUT DO OTHER THINGS TOO

Some people's lives revolve exclusively around food. The same thing can happen with sex. Sex is a very important part of marriage, but not the most important part. Married couples with fulfilling sex lives have good communication, resolve conflict, enjoy activities, together, have healthy friendships with others, and a variety of other factors that allow them to come to their spouse as a fuller person.

## MR. AND MRS. SOLOMON'S STORY

Literature records many great love affairs, but none are as ancient and passionate as the relationship between the man and woman in the biblical book of Song of Songs. With richly suggestive imagery, the author tells the story of a young man and woman in their mutual pursuit of each other. The song describes interactions between him, her, and a chorus of friends as the two express their romantic and sensual desire for one another. The book has caused no small amount of flushed faces in religious circles, leading many to believe the erotic poem is allegorical—telling of God's *agape* love for humanity. But a plain reading of the song clearly points to a sexualized story of two people enraptured in love.

The song serves as a biblical endorsement of marital bliss and sexual satisfaction. Tradition records them as Solomon and the Shulammite (loosely translated Mr. and Mrs. Solomon). Their story has inspired centuries of lovers to fully delight in God's gift of sex. It is not directly explicit. The book uses pastoral imagery for sexual references (such as gardens, fruits, and flowers). It is also not a how-to manual for sex, but rather a story of lovers who knew how-to enjoy themselves.[20]

What was their secret?

## THEY AFFIRMED AND PRAISED EACH OTHER

The Solomons loved each other and made sure it was clearly known. There was no doubt in their minds of what the other thought of them—physically. Three separate places in the book record what are called *wasfs* or description songs of the lovers to each other. Solomon looks at his bride and praises how she looks from her head down: eyes, hair, teeth, lips, neck, and breasts (4:1–7), and later from the feet up (7:1–5). He doesn't miss saying something wonderful about every part he sees. She has a similar praise of him, telling him and herself that she likes what she sees. She finds ways to celebrate his face, arms, legs, and body or torso (5:10–16). When it is so easy to give in to insecurity, self-doubt, and comparisons, this couple modeled the importance of verbally affirming and praising one's lover's physical appearance.

## THEY OVERCAME OBSTACLES TO INTIMACY

With closeness and love come risks and problems. Halfway through the song, a dream is recorded. She is asleep in bed, and he comes to the bed chamber wanting sex. She refuses him using a variety of reasons. He tries harder to persuade her. In the end, she unlocks the door having a changed heart and readied for passion, only to find him gone (5:1–8). Though we don't know how this night of different desires was resolved, we know that this couple was intentional about dealing with problems before they got worse. Solomon says earlier, "Catch for us the foxes, the little foxes that ruin the vineyards, our vineyards that are in bloom" (2:15).

In poetic wisdom, he saw that little things could ruin big things. He wanted to address problems, however small, which would intrude on their sexual intimacy.

> God does not sugarcoat the subject of sex in his word. He knows that along with the delight of sexual intimacy also come difficulties. . . . If we want to live as servant lovers and forge a vital marriage despite problems and challenges, we must continue to make sacrificial choices.
> —Joseph and Linda Dillow

## THEY COMMUNICATED DESIRE

If there is one thing Mr. and Mrs. Solomon can be credited for, it is being very clear about when they wanted each other. The invitations to sex which they provide one another in the poem are as arousing as they are beautiful. It is after hearing her husband praise her physical beauty—and indicating that he wanted to "go to the mountain of myrrh" (4:6) that she gives him a formal invitation to her body. "Awake, north wind, and come, south wind! Blow on my garden, that its fragrance may spread abroad. Let my lover come into his garden and taste its choice fruits" (4:16).

She later implies to her chorus of friends that her husband is regularly invited to "brows[e] among the lilies" (6:3). He also lets his desire be known. After verbally praising her physical beauty, this man of the desert describes her body as a fertile palm tree that he would like to climb in order to "take hold of its fruit" (see 7:6–9). They fully explored the many ways they could communicate sexual desire to one another.

## THEY TIMED THEIR PASSION

The poem progresses from admiration, attraction, and affirmation to commitment, consummation, and celebration. There is a tension in their story of fully enjoying their sexual union and restraining the power of sexual love when needed. The poem's transition in chapter 3 records Mrs. Solomon basking in the beauty of a wedding ceremony. She is either remembering her own or enjoying a procession passing by. Her delight indicates the importance of marital commitment. The often quoted, "Do not arouse or awaken love until it so desires" (3:5), speaks of the lovers' own view that passionate and erotic love should be treated like fire—something to be enjoyed as well as protected and respected.

> She warns the others not to arouse love until they are ready to meet its rigors, both physical and emotional. Love is not a passing fling but rather a demanding and exhausting relationship.
> —Tremper Longman III

Sex and sexuality is a gift of God. *Eros*, the third kind of love in marriage, is God's way of binding a man and woman who have committed themselves to a spiritual relationship with God and each other and have found a faithful friendship and a partner for life.

*Eternal Spirit,*

*We thank you for the gift of physical love and passion. You have made sex to connect us on a deeper level. As we sort through all the messages in our world, help us to understand and live out the truth found in your Word. As we commit to each other for life, may we enjoy the wonderful pleasures you allow, resist the temptations of our selfishness, and serve each other in love—soul and body.*

*In Jesus' Name,*
*Amen*

## DISCUSSION STARTERS

1. What do you believe was most important in this chapter?

2. After reading this chapter, what (if anything) do you and your spouse have different beliefs about? In what areas are your beliefs and values about sex similar?

3. Where (and from whom) did you first learn about sex? Was what you learned accurate? Was it biblical?

4. In what ways have you or your spouse experienced sexual brokenness? Are any of the following in your personal sexual history: use or abuse of pornography, sexual abuse, rape, unwanted sexual experiences early in life, sex-guilt from previous relationships? In what ways have you sought or found healing from these experiences?

5. Read through Les and Leslie Parrot's ten stages of intimacy listed on pages 117–118. What number has your relationship progressed to? At what point should a couple be married before experiencing the next stage of intimacy?

## LOVE IN ACTION

1. Make a commitment to God and a trusted friend (of the same gender and similar values) that you will conform as closely as possible to God's plan for sexual intimacy, which includes sexual purity before marriage and faithfulness within marriage. Give permission to that person to hold you accountable, including asking you about your thought life and behaviors regarding your sexuality.

2. Make a list of three ways you have or will invite God into your sex life. Make another list of attitudes or behaviors that have (or could) hinder you from experiencing God's blessing in the bedroom. Discuss those lists with your spouse. Come up with a plan of how you can encourage the first list to happen and prevent the second list from happening.

3. If you struggle with Internet pornography or sense this could be problem, download a filter and accountability software for your computer, such as the one found at covenanteyes.com. If you experienced some form of sexual abuse, consider reading a Christian book on the subject to explore how this may affect present or future intimacy. I highly recommend *The Wounded Heart* by Dan Allender.

4. If you are married, reserve an hour of time together. Get naked and take turns verbally affirming each other's bodies. State specific body parts of your spouse that you find attractive and

desirable. Touch and explore those parts as you describe them. Allow the time to progress in a way that is comfortable to you both.

## RECOMMENDED READING

*The Gift of Sex: A Guide to Sexual Fulfillment* by Clifford and Joyce Penner

*Intimacy Ignited: Conversations Couple to Couple: Fire Up Your Sex Life with the Song of Solomon* by Joseph and Linda Dillow and Peter and Lorraine Pintus

*Sacred Influence: How God Uses Wives to Shape the Souls of Their Husbands* by Gary Thomas

*The Way to Love Your Wife: Creating Greater Love & Passion in the Bedroom* by Clifford and Joyce Penner

# BECOMING ONE

Love at first sight is easy to understand; it's when two people
have been looking at each other for a lifetime that it becomes a miracle.
—Amy Bloom[1]

> We rejoice and delight in you; we will praise your love more than wine.
> —Song of Songs 1:4

How does this all work?

How can we know which love is best at different times?

How can we be brother and sister, friends, and lovers at the same time?

It was obvious that Marie's heart was heavy. She had something to tell me but didn't know how to begin.

"I need to talk to my brother in Christ," she said.

In my mind, I pretended like we were back in college. I tried to posture myself like I was her best friend—not married to her, not living under the same roof, not sleeping with her. She continued . . .

"I spent more than I should on the credit card, and I feel horrible."

It was early on in our marriage, and we had been struggling financially. We had made an agreement about saving and spending. We were also trying to communicate better about money. Marie needed me to see that while she knew she had disappointed her husband, she really felt like she had disappointed herself and God. She did not need a husband wondering how much of "his" money she had spent. She needed her Christian brother who could hear her confession and offer God's grace and support.

I usually end this story with a funny statement like, "She was smart to say who she wanted to talk to because her husband was ticked! Maybe she should have asked for her husband to stay out of the room while she talked to her brother in Christ!" All joking aside, she wasn't being manipulative; she was being strategic. She gave me a simple cue to let me know how I should interpret what she wanted to tell me. I found it very helpful. There's a name for it in communication theory—*code switching*.

## CODE SWITCHING

In linguistics, code switching is when people change from speaking one language to another. People who can speak multiple languages do this all the time. Maybe the person to whom they are speaking understands one language, but someone new to the conversation knows another. Sometimes there are words or phrases that are best understood in one language more than the other. My wife code switches when she speaks with some of her family. Vietnamese is their first language and sometimes it is easier for them to understand each other in that language instead of English. There are also many subtle cultural connections made when they speak Vietnamese rather than English.

In *Code Switching: How to Talk So Men Will Listen*, Drs. Claire Brown and Audrey Nelson define a code switch as "the ability to use your knowledge of two or more cultures or languages and switch between them, depending on the situation, in order to best communicate your message."[2]

Code switching is about choosing words, language, and other signals to help us connect with another person. It's about using your knowledge of the other person in order to choose the best way to communicate with them. Understanding the situation and your knowledge of the other person can help you decide how to accomplish your goal in communicating.

In the same way that people code switch between languages given the situation and their goals, we can code switch between the three different kinds of love—*agape*, *philia*, and *eros* to connect and communicate with our mate. There are situations when one kind of love is the better way to communicate than the others. How do we know which kind of love is best for a situation?

The first step is to consider your goal. Here are a few questions to ask: What do I want to communicate? Given what I know about my mate, which kind of love will best communicate this? Is this the best time to express this kind of love?

Let me illustrate. Let's say I want to communicate to my wife how incredibly thankful I am to be married to her and how I want to spend the rest of my life with her. I want to communicate *agape* and *philia* love. The first thing that goes through my mind is walking up behind her, holding her in a tight embrace and nuzzling my face in her black flowing hair. Knowing my wife, she would read this as *eros* and assume I'm making a move on her. Being attentive to her stories, giving her encouraging words, and praying for her verbalized needs would be the best way to love her with *agape* and *philia* love.

It's important to not only know which expression of love should be chosen to send the message you want, but also which expression of love your spouse needs at the time. The more you get to know your spouse, the better you will be at code switching to the best expression of love. But how do I know what kind of love my spouse needs?

Learn the cues. When Marie and I first began to apply this idea of code switching, it was very direct and verbal.

"I have a spiritual struggle. I want to talk to you as my sister in Christ."

"We'd benefit from some friendship time. What do you want to do?"

"That lover part of our relationship is something I've missed lately."

Over time, we have learned how to pick up small cues to discern which expression of love would be best at the time. Those small cues may involve code words, meaningful touches, and gestures that say what kind of love is being requested or given. I believe women tend to be more sensitive to which expressions of love are best in different situations. Marie is really good about this with us. For example, when I share a difficult situation I am facing, she seems to know which would be the best response to my challenge—praying for me, giving me a friendly "attaboy," or reminding me that I am her man with a passionate kiss.

Code switching looks different for each couple. However it looks, the goal is the same—to send a message to the other person that lets him or her know what kind of love is being expressed. Here are some examples:

- A Catholic couple I met kissed each other three times before going to sleep at night. The husband said it was his way of saying to his wife, "I love you in the name of the Father, the Son, and the Holy Spirit." His wife knew that if he kissed her three times, she was supposed to understand that a different way than if he kissed her once. The third kiss was a code switch to *agape*.

- I know a serious, devout couple that gives each other high fives at home. Their jobs and ministry commitments are demanding and they take what they do seriously. But when one hand goes up in the air inviting a slap from the other, it's their way of saying to each other, "We're a great team, and I love you." They'll often do this at times of great stress and pressure. It's their way of reminding each other that they are friends. A raised don't-leave-me-hanging hand in the air communicates *philia*.

- One couple I met told me that they have code words for sex that they can use in public settings. The wife told me, "Sometimes we say, 'We have to go home and do some laundry' or I say 'We have to go; John has some work to do before bed.'" Whether they were in the middle of a light conversation with friends or talking casually after a Bible study, a simple code switch signaled the *eros* awakening.

How do you communicate to your spouse that you love him or her as God does? How do you remind each other of your friendship? How do you send the message of sexual desire to your mate? Couples should talk about what kind of love certain cues are intended to communicate. The more we understand the different kinds of love and the more we understand our spouse, the better we will be at discerning how to best love them at different times and situations.

## EBB AND FLOW

At different times in our relationship, one expression of love may be more important than the other. Consider the following times in the life of a relationship:

- Dating
- Engagement or preparing for marriage

- Newlyweds
- Illness or serious life transitions
- Crisis in your religious community or questioning faith issues
- Death in the family
- Birth of a child
- Loss of a child
- Job change or relocation
- Body changes affecting sexuality (such as menopause or blood pressure issues)
- Grown children leaving the home
- Changes in lifestyle due to advanced aging

Given the circumstances of life, you may find *agape*, *philia*, or *eros* more important than the others. This is the ebb and flow of love. Working together to discover which kind of love serves the relationship best is an important part of becoming one and working toward a lifelong union.

Here are a few examples of love at different times of life.

AGAPE

David and Rachel knew they were meant for each other but couldn't figure out how to recover from David's recent infidelity. They had struggled with intimacy issues throughout their twenty-year marriage. After the infidelity, they realized they were more spiritually similar than spiritually intimate. They had the same spiritual convictions, were actively involved in the same church, and enjoyed the same kind of spiritual music. They also hid their true spiritual struggles in the same way. Deeply hurting, they secretly struggled with guilt from past decisions, shame, and the belief that, if they opened up about what they were really dealing with, it would be disastrous. The infidelity forced them to find a new way. "I need to know that my husband is following God in order for me to trust him again," Rachel said. "And I know there is some stuff I need the Lord to change in me. I'd like us to be spiritual partners in this." In the pain of a serious breach of trust, loyalty and selfless love are essential. *Agape* should be David and Rachel's primary expression of love as they rebuild trust.

## PHILIA

Nicole's business trips were an important part of her growing career. There were so many people seeking her consulting expertise that she was turning down new clients. She and Daniel knew that it wouldn't be forever, but it was creating more stress on their young relationship. Newly engaged and planning a wedding, they were concerned that they were missing each other at a crucial time in their relationship. With all their commitments, they only saw each other once a week, if that. In hopes of getting more time together, they thought about moving in together. After thinking it through, they concluded that it wouldn't give them what they really wanted—time to connect. "We're not stupid. It would be about sex, not talking,"

Daniel said. "Instead of saving on rent, we spent more on cell phone hours and found a way to chat online. I'm shocked," Daniel said embarrassedly, "how much you talk about so many amazing things and find out so much about a person when groping them is not an option!" Daniel and Nicole were experiencing *philia*, a friendship that would keep the love alive in their relationship long beyond schedule challenges.

EROS

Gus and Therese worked hard to keep their spiritual relationship and friendship strong through their twenty years of active parenting. They were committed leaders in their church and made sure they found time for activities together like bike riding to a restaurant at the beach where they would enjoy long talks over lunch. What was always an area of growth was their sexual intimacy. They had a regular schedule for sex, but it was at the end of their busy days—when the best of themselves had already been given away to kids, school, and ministry at church. That all changed when the last child moved out. "There have been different seasons in our relationship," Therese said. "We love each other and are great friends and partners. But lately," she said with a knowing smile at Gus, "It's been fun having the freedom to be more sexual with each other! It's a great thing to look forward to." Having been faithful and committed to a common mission and purpose for years, a new chapter was opening for Gus and Therese. *Eros* would be an important expression of their love at this stage in life.

Code switching between *agape*, *philia*, and *eros*. can only work when the other person is ready to receive it. Have you ever spoken to someone and then realized they did not speak your language? How about telling a joke only to get the response that they were not in the mood for humor? Just like the only successful throws in baseball are the ones that are caught, the only successful code switches are the ones when both people are in agreement. The ancient wisdom of the Bible says that *philia* is demonstrated as we seek to put the other person's needs above our own: "Be devoted to one another in brotherly love. Honor one another above yourselves" (Rom. 12:10).

Two people in a relationship can be at very different places with very different needs. What expression of love would best serve your mate right now? What expression of love is best for your relationship?

## FINDING THE CENTER

Ideally, as we grow in becoming one, we express these forms of love more fluidly. There is an ebb and flow between *agape*, *philia*, and *eros*. We praise God while having sex and explore our spiritual struggles during a friendly game of tennis. As we become one, our love is more unified, not compartmentalized. The following image shows how all three loves overlap.

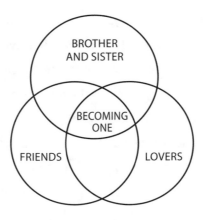

How do we find the center? I believe it happens as we get to know one another and plan our lives together based on that knowledge. Author and marriage expert Dennis Rainey writes, "One of the riskiest, but most rewarding benefits of a marriage relationship is the exhilarating experience of knowing and being known, of revealing and having another person reveal themselves to you."[3]

To know someone deeply is a very intimate experience. The Hebrew word *yadah* means to have knowledge of someone or to be known. The word is also used for sexual relations.[4] The most literal way of translating Genesis 4:1 is: "Adam knew his wife; and she conceived." To "know" someone is to have a personal intimate knowledge of them and live in a way that reflects that knowledge. Much of this kind of knowledge comes from years of living together, laboring through the challenges of life, and partnering in life opportunities.

But great things can be accomplished by getting an accurate assessment of the relationship.

I highly recommend a great assessment tool called Prepare-Enrich.[5] It is a comprehensive, accurate, and reliable couple evaluation that includes skill-building exercises for premarital couples and those looking to improve their marriages. It includes personality, family of origin, and individual assessment scales including:

- Communication
- Conflict resolution
- Partner style and habits
- Financial management
- Leisure activities
- Sexual expectations
- Family and friends
- Relationship roles
- Spiritual beliefs

To be successful in our careers, we need to be knowledgeable of our specific job, the customers or clients, and the culture in which we work, as well as keeping up with the latest changes and challenges in the field. The same is true in marriage. Unfortunately, if our marriages were our jobs, many of us would have been fired long ago. Some of us have been.

Marie and I went through this program and then created a three-year plan to work on the growth areas identified by the assessment. Prepare-Enrich requires a trained facilitator, but it is well worth the cost and interaction. Many churches, synagogues, and counselors are equipped to help you get the assessment and create a plan based on what you learn. In a culture in which over 50 percent of marriages end in divorce, and second marriages are at an even higher risk,[6] I have found a good assessment and plan is instrumental in helping couples work to find the center of their love.

## THE GREATEST OF THESE

There are different times and seasons in which one kind of love needs to take center stage.

Sometimes you need to pray more than play.

Sometimes sex needs to take a backseat to friendship.

Sometimes the Bible needs to be put down, and you need some time in bed.

We need all three kinds of love to make a marriage work. One informs the next. But the greatest love is the love that flows from heaven into our relationships—love that not only lasts a lifetime, but transcends time itself. Despite the romantic notions we have about our marriages lasting forever, Jesus taught that in heaven there is no marriage (Matt. 22:23–33). It begs the question: "What kind of love can I experience that will last for eternity?"

C. S. Lewis writes that the love one could experience with one's spouse for eternity would depend on "what kind of love it had become, or was becoming, on earth."[7] Sexual love ends because these bodies in which we reside end. Friendship is wonderful, but it, too, has a limited life span. Friends are allies in life, but death brings an end to all friendships—unless there is a greater love. It is the love of spiritual siblings that continues forever. When we are partners in marriage under God, that partnership never ends. Husband and wife who are spiritual brother and sister continue to be spiritual brother and sister throughout eternity. That's all the more reason to choose *agape* over all other kinds of love. Lewis writes:

> Suppose you are fortunate enough to have "fallen in love with" and married your Friend. And now suppose it possible that you were offered the choice of two futures: "Either you two will cease to be lovers but remain forever joint seekers of the same God, the same beauty, the same truth, or else, losing all that, you will retain as long as you live the raptures and ardours, all wonder and the wild desire of Eros. Choose which you please." Which should we choose? Which choice should we not regret after we had made it?[8]

What does it mean to choose *agape* above all other loves? It means that, if we want to have love of an eternal quality, we need to look to the only One that exists for eternity. How can we know how to love without having experienced love by love's Creator? This is how Jesus' beloved friend said it:

This is how God showed his love for us: God sent his only Son into the world so we might live through him. This is the kind of love we are talking about—not that we once upon a time loved God, but that he loved us and sent his Son as a sacrifice to clear away our sins and the damage they've done to our relationship with God. My dear, dear friends, if God loved us like this, we certainly ought to love each other. No one has seen God, ever. But if we love one another, God dwells deeply within us, and his love becomes complete in us—perfect love! (1 John 4:9–12 MSG)

God is love. That's where it starts. Marie and I have found that in our greatest times of hardship, imitating God's selfless love has been of greatest value. We believe that Jesus' sacrifice on the cross is not only the way we can experience the power to love and forgive, but it is also the greatest model of selfless love.

Love. What does it mean?

Love is about a selfless commitment to another person that is rooted in a spiritual bond. Love is about a being a companion in life with someone we enjoy. Love is about giving ourselves sexually to someone who we wildly trust. It is mature and thoughtful, not rash and rapturous. It is passionate but not before its time.

We need a new view of love, which is actually an old understanding. The ancients had it right. When they looked at love, they saw three kinds: "I take pleasure in three things and they are beautiful in the sight of God and of mortals: agreement among brothers and sisters, friendship among neighbors, and a wife and a husband who live in harmony."[9]

It is my prayer that you would experience all three of the loves written about in these pages in all their fullness. May you find, now and in the future, that the Lord of creation, companionship, and the cross is at the center of your marriage.

*God of Love,*

*Thank you for giving a vision for the kind of love you want in our lives. Thank you for the deep and powerful love of* eros *which allows us to celebrate your creation of our wonderfully made bodies. Thank you for the rich and delightful bond of* philia *which grants us allies and partners in the pleasures and challenges of our earthly lives. And thank you most of all for* agape, *your love for us. That love gives us a picture of how to selflessly love others. As we open our hearts to you, your love offers us a way to experience forgiveness of our sins and a sure future with you and all those who love you when this life ends. May your love guide ours.*

*In Jesus' Name,*
*Amen*

## DISCUSSION STARTERS

1. What do you believe was most important in this chapter?

2. After reading this chapter, what (if anything) do you and your spouse have different beliefs about? In what areas are your beliefs and values similar?

3. Can you find examples of code switching in your life?

4. Of the different possible circumstances in a relationship listed on pages 139–140, write down which kind of love might best serve your spouse's needs and the needs of the relationship—*agape*, *philia*, or *eros*. What would that love look like in practical terms? You do not need to come to an agreement. Discuss the differences you discover.

5. What are the three strongest areas of your relationship? What are three areas in which growth is needed? Discuss the differences in your lists.

## LOVE IN ACTION

1. Identify and write down three times when you have attempted to code switch in your relationship. What kind of love were you trying to communicate—*agape*, *philia*, or *eros*? What was a cue or signal that one kind of love was being requested? Was it verbal or nonverbal? Was the signal understood? Discuss what might be clearer—words, cues, or signals—in the future.

2. Make a list of times when you have experienced being spiritual siblings, friends, and lovers. Write out the words, actions, or attitudes that made it clear that it was *agape*, *philia*, or *eros*. Which of these comes most naturally to you as a couple? Which may take more work to improve?

3. Plan a date that mixes two kinds of love together. Discuss how each kind of love was expressed and how you felt about them overlapping.

4. Log onto prepare-enrich.com, and locate a facilitator to assist you in taking an assessment. Then create a plan to work on growth areas in your relationship.

# RECOMMENDED READING

*The 5 Love Languages: The Secret to Love That Lasts* by Gary Chapman

*For Men Only: A Straightforward Guide to the Inner Lives of Women* by Shaunti and Jeff Feldhahn

*For Women Only: What You Need to Know about the Inner Lives of Men* by Shaunti Feldhahn

*Preparing for Marriage* by David Boehi, Brent Nelson, Jeff Schulte, and Lloyd Shadrach

# NOTES

## INTRODUCTION

1. Aristotle, *Nicomachean Ethics*, Book 8, trans. David Ross (Oxford, England: Oxford University Press, 1980). Also available at pages.interlog.com/~girbe/ethics8.html, accessed July 9, 2010.
2. C. S. Lewis, *The Four Loves* (New York: Harcourt, 1960).
3. Mark Twain, accessed January 4, 2010, www.cmgww.com/historic/twain/about/quotes2.htm.

## CHAPTER 1

1. Craig Glickman, *Solomon's Song of Love* (West Monroe, La.: Howard Publishing, 2004), 28.
2. *Aesop's Fables* (New York: Barnes and Noble Books, 2003), 17.
3. By "interfaith," I am referring to people of two different religions (for example, Muslim and Christian) as opposed to "*intra*faith," which refers to people of differing beliefs within the same religion (for example, Baptist Christianity and Methodist Christianity). In both cases, religious differences are highly important in assessing

spiritual compatibility. The website, www.religioustolerance.org/ifm_menu.htm, has a wide variety of information on this complex issue. While exploring the statistics and anecdotal evidence, it's clear that religious beliefs alone are not the only issue. Nevertheless, the website concludes: "Most of the data seems to show that religious differences within inter-faith and intra-faith marriages is a major contributor to marriage breakdown. If nothing else, it at least should impress on a couple entering such a relationship that they need to pay close attention to resolving religious difference" (www.religious tolerance.org/ifm_divo.htm).

4. Les Parrott and Leslie Parrott, *Saving Your Marriage Before It Starts: Seven Questions to Ask Before and After You Marry* (Grand Rapids, Mich.: Zondervan, 2006), 142. An important clarification comes from John Gottman's research. Gottman is less concerned with agreement on specific religious teachings. Rather, he looks for how those beliefs are played out in daily life. See John Gottman, *The Seven Principles for Making Marriage Work* (New York: Three Rivers Press, 2000).

5. Gary Thomas, *Devotions for a Sacred Marriage: A Year of Weekly Devotions for Couples* (Grand Rapids, Mich.: Zondervan, 2005), 21.

6. Jan Baird, e-mail message to author, August 7, 2009.

7. Sue Edwards, Kelley Mathews, and Henry J. Rogers, *Mixed Ministry: Working Together as Brothers and Sisters in an Oversexed Society* (Grand Rapids, Mich.: Kregel, 2008), 108–110.

8. Elisabeth Dodds, *Marriage to a Difficult Man: The Uncommon Union of Jonathan and Sarah Edwards* (Philadelphia, Pa.: Westminster Press, 1971), 38.

9. Ibid., 7

10. Ibid., 35.

11. Ibid., 201.

CHAPTER 2

1. John Gottman, *The Seven Principles for Making Marriage Work* (New York: Three Rivers Press, 2000), 19.

2. *Boston Legal*, "On the Ledge," originally aired November 28, 2006, http://bostonlegal.wetpaint.com/page/3x09+on+The+Ledge.

3. Gottman, 48.

4. "Popular," accessed July 9, 2010, www.stlyrics.com/songs/w/wicked22494/popular1009595.html.

5. Willard F. Harley, Jr., *His Needs, Her Needs: Building an Affair-Proof Marriage* (Grand Rapids, Mich.: Fleming H. Revell Publisher, 1999), 75–87.

6. Robert Mark Kamen, *The Karate Kid* original screenplay, accessed July 9, 2010, http://www.awesomefilm.com/script/karatekid.pdf.

7. Tom Rath, *Vital Friends: The People You Can't Afford to Live Without* (New York: Gallup Press, 2006), 33–38.

8. Mark Galli, "My Wife's Worst Girlfriend," accessed July 9, 2010, http://www.kyria.com/topics/marriagefamily/marriage/spirituality/mywifesworstgirlfriend.html?start=3.

9. Teri Engle, personal telephone conversation with author, October 20, 2009.

10. Florence Isaacs, *Toxic Friends, True Friends* (New York: Kesington Press, 1999), 64.

11. Rath, 105.

12. Margaret A. Hogan and C. James Taylor, eds., *My Dearest Friends: Letters of Abigail and John Adams* (Cambridge, Mass.: Belknap Press, 2007), 91.

13. Ibid., 12.

## CHAPTER 3

1. Jerry D. Hardin and Dianne C. Sloan, *Getting Ready for Marriage Workbook: How to Really Get to Know the Person You're Going to Marry* (Nashville: Thomas Nelson, 1992), 218–219.
2. Hugh Hefner, accessed July 10, 2010, http://thinkexist.com/quotes/hugh_hefner/.
3. Advertising slogan for Hustler Stores, popularly attributed to Hustler founder, Larry Flint.
4. Mark Laaser, *Healing the Wounds of Sexual Addiction* (Grand Rapids, Mich.: Zondervan, 2004), 15.
5. Rape, Abuse, Incest National Network, "Statistics," accessed July 10, 2010, http://www.rainn.org/statistics.
6. Marion Goertz, "Sexuality and the Human Condition," accessed July 10, 2010, http://www.canadiantherapists.com/Marion Goertz/Sexuality_Human_Condition.pdf.
7. Ibid.
8. Ibid.
9. Personal and confidential e-mail message to author, July 9, 2009.
10. Joyce Penner, personal telephone conversation with author, February 17, 2010.
11. Denise Foley and Eileen Nechas, *Women's Encyclopedia of Health & Emotional Healing: Top Women Doctors Share Their Unique Self-Help Advice on Your Body, Your Feelings, and Your Life* (Emmaus, Pa.: Rodale Press, 1993), 128.
12. Penner, telephone conversation.
13. Mike McManus and Harriet McManus, *Living Together: Myths, Risks & Answers* (New York: Howard Books, 2008), 9.
14. The problem of and solutions for sexual ambivalence are discussed in detail by Clifford Penner and Joyce Penner in *Restoring the*

Pleasure: Complete Step-by-Step Programs to Help Couples Overcome the Most Common Sexual Barriers (Nashville: W Publishing Group, 1993), 223–225. Special thanks to Joyce Penner for taking the time to help clarify this issue with me when reviewing the chapter.

15. Jennifer Crittenden, "The Apology," *Seinfeld*, season 9, episode 9, directed by Andy Ackerman, aired December 11, 1997, accessed July 15, 2010, http://www.seinology.com/scripts/ script-165.shtml.

16. Joseph Henry Thayer, *The New Thayer's Greek-English Lexicon* (Peabody, Mass.: Hendrickson, 1981), 122.

17. C. S. Lewis, *The Four Loves* (New York: Harcourt, 1960), 104.

18. Les Parrott and Leslie Parrott, *Relationships* (Grand Rapids, Mich.: Zondervan, 1998), 137.

19. Taken from various resources of Clifford and Joyce Penner, including personal conversations and their DVD series: The Magic & Mystery of Sex.

20. For an engaging and practical couple's study through Song of Songs, I recommend Joseph and Linda Dillow and Peter and Lorraine Pintus, *Intimacy Ignited: Conversations Couple to Couple: Fire Up Your Sex Life with the Song of Solomon* (Colorado Springs: NavPress, 2004). The Mr. and Mrs. Solomon reference is from them.

CHAPTER 4

1. Amy Bloom, accessed July 15, 2010, http://www.goodreads.com/author/quotes/115220.Amy_Bloom.

2. Claire Damken Brown and Audrey Nelson, *Code Switching: How to Talk So Men Will Listen* (New York: Penguin Books, 2009), viii. Another helpful idea related to this is Communication Accommodation Theory or CAT, which suggests that code switching occurs when two people want to emphasize similarities between them (see more

about this at http://en.wikipedia.org/wiki/Communication_ Accommodation_Theory).

3. David Boehi et al., Dennis Rainey, ed., *Preparing for Marriage* (Ventura, Calif.: Gospel Light, 1997), 17.

4. Francis Brown, S. R. Driver, and Charles A. Briggs, *The New Brown-Driver-Briggs-Gesenius Hebrew English Lexicon* (Peabody, Mass.: Hendrickson, 1979), 394.

5. Life Innovations, Inc., "Prepare-Enrich," accessed July 20, 2010, http://www.prepare-enrich.com.

6. Les Parrot and Leslie Parrot, *Saving Your Second Marriage before It Starts* (Grand Rapids, Mich.: Zondervan, 2001), 12.

7. C. S. Lewis, *The Four Loves* (New York: Harcourt, 1960), 137.

8. Ibid., 67–68.

9. Sirach 25:1 (NRSV). I've included this passage because it so eloquently displays the three-fold view of relationships in the ancient world. *Sirach* is also known as the *Wisdom of Ben Sira* or *Ecclesiasticus*. It is not considered inspired Scripture by Protestants, but is included in the Bibles of Catholics and most Orthodox Christians and is quoted in the Talmud and rabbinic literature. Special thanks to Dr. Joe Hellerman for helping me locate the best translation of this passage.